The Honeymoon Habit

Lessons for Renewing Romance and Reconnecting with Your Spouse

TONY GARASCIA, MS, LCSW

ISBN: 1-4392-0635-X
ISBN-13: 9781439206355

Visit www.booksurge.com to order additional copies.

TABLE OF CONTENTS

To Beth, who has kept the passion
and imagination alive and has made
the journey all the better.

INTRODUCTION

Live the life you've imagined," says the ad. Can you remember the life you imagined back in the days of your courtship? Are you living it now? In those days, before children, before the mortgage, even before you started planning your wedding, there was more time to talk about your life together, to dream about the future, and to imagine what your life would be someday. Now that the future has arrived, you may find it harder to carve out time for dreaming. The pressures of work, the harried pace of caring for a growing family, and the ups and downs of the daily routine can leave little time for anything but the most basic conversations about practical matters, never mind the sharing of hopes and expectations.

But when you met and fell in love and began to talk seriously about spending your future with one another, you began to form images in your minds that gave you a picture of how your life would turn out. Often, these images involved a good deal of love and unity, and provided the energy that propelled you to take the next step of proclaiming to family and friends your intent to be married. If an older family member questioned you about how you would handle future crises and problems, you probably said, "We'll work it out somehow," or, "Our love will get us through." When two people start their married life, it's almost like they look up at the starry sky with wonder and amazement, with a mixture of gratitude and fear, but most of all with hope in the future.

This book is intended to help you continue the conversation about your relationship that started during your courtship. I hope it will enable you to sustain the original energy that propelled you forward, to marry and to begin a family together. Perhaps that energy has waned and it's time to rekindle it.

Many who work with married couples today tend to focus on helping them improve their basic skills, skills like communicating or problem solving. Such basic skills certainly are essential. But marriage is much more than a skill set. It is an act of the imagination.

Some say it is our imagination that is the uniquely human part of us. Through our imaginations we anticipate our future by dreaming about it, and the images we construct of ourselves in our future are a significant means of planning for the future. The young person who has a dream of being a doctor constructs images of what that will be like. It is usually these images that sustain the individual when the going gets tough or when the dream is tested. Sometimes we doubt our dreams and may think that our imaging has failed us. And, of course, our imagination is not based on pure fantasy but has to go through its own "reality testing" where our hopes and dreams of the future are tempered and changed by the realities of everyday life.

The idea of marriage as an act of imagination offers us a way to "remember the future." In the days of your courtship as you dreamed about the future, you didn't focus on the skills you would need to make your marriage work. You dreamed instead of being lovers, partners, companions, and friends. These images—lover, partner, companion, and friend—are the core images that serve as the organizing energy points of your marriage. These images are what sustain you when the going gets tough or when your dreams are tested. Remembering these original images can propel you to the future.

I have used these four images in my own marriage therapy with couples and can attest to the deep resonance that couples experience when they are presented with them. Each of these four images has both a secular and religious dimension and can be found in the secular literature of love as well as in the scriptures of many religions.

The four images, taken as imaginative catalysts that can sustain a marriage, can be presented as a series of propositions:

- When we marry we join together each believing the other will be with and for them a lover, a partner, a companion, and a friend.

- At every major transition in our life as a couple each of these images has to be revisited and imaged anew by us.
- All of them, taken together, will sustain a marriage. One without the others will sustain a marriage for a time but cannot alone carry a marriage into the future.
- The skills we learn that have to do with communication and problem solving are the means we use to sustain these images over time.

Imagination and spirituality go hand in hand. It is our imaginations that impel us to ask spiritual questions—questions about the meaning and purpose of life, about suffering and death, about coping with our limits and failures, our questions. And it is our imaginations that lead us to place ourselves in another's shoes and have empathy for those who suffer. As we engage in this process we draw from the spirituality that our religious traditions offer us and engage in the creation of a unique spirituality for our marriage. The spiritual source that this book draws primarily from is the Judeo-Christian tradition, although other sources are occasionally employed. We begin by focusing on the relationship between two spouses and the importance of intimacy; then we explore the four images of married love, and then move onto skills and other essential ingredients of marriage. In each chapter the spiritual dimension is brought into focus along with a few questions to prime the pump of your own spiritual imagination.

Each chapter can be read in a ten to fifteen minute period. It is my hope that this book will be read equally by men and women. The brevity of the chapters is intended to facilitate discussion between you. The chapters can also be used by small groups of married people for enrichment or discussion purposes. Each chapter has a set of questions meant to start the conversation. The aim of these questions is to offer you some positive steps you can take to make your marriage better.

Each chapter also has a "Real Life" section that presents a particular problem that a married couple might encounter. These life illustrations are fictional renderings of problems that married couples often encounter. While my experience as a marriage therapist has been helpful in knowing the territory of marriage problems, it is important to note that they are not case studies as such and no case notes were consulted in the construction of them. If you recognize your experience in any of the illustrations then I have done my job well.

Skills are important, especially during the years when your time and energy are so engaged in raising a family. And while this book will place a good deal of emphasis on these skills, I hope it will always help you to remember that marriage is more than a set of skills. More importantly, I hope it will encourage you to use your imagination to find new ways to grow as lovers, partners, companions, and friends.

MARRIAGE QUEST

An archaeologist is the best
husband any woman can
have: the older she gets, the
more interested he is in her.
– AGATHA CHRISTIE

Imagine going on a journey that has adventure, peril, appeal and even times of boredom. It is a long journey with many challenges. As you begin this quest, like in any quest, you need good friends, tools and supplies for the journey, and some sense of where you are headed. You need people to cover your back and there will be times when you are called to cover your partner's back. And your tools, like any tools of a fantasy game, will be the tools of your talents, your wit, your ability to solve conflict and communicate what you need and want; most important, this quest will take you through many transitions, where you will morph from young to older, from less mature to more mature. In these transition points, you will be asked to make basic decisions about how to survive, decisions like how to take care of yourself physically and financially, decisions about your mental and over all well being. And, oh yes, there will be a lot of passion in this quest provided you make the right decisions during your transition.

Marriage is a quest for friendship, intimacy, love and a lasting partnership that thrives many years. Unfortunately today, many people don't see marriage as a journey quest but more as a state of boredom where people are allowed to step off the line of taking care of their bodies and their emotional, physical, sexual and spiritual selves. Marriage doesn't have to be like this, but we let it become this way by becoming less, not more disciplined, in the quest. In the beginning many people have lofty goals and dreams for their relationships, but often these dreams fail to materialize due to a failure to master the essential skills of the journey quest of marriage. Skills like renewal of the self, empathic communication and coaching, consistent and respectful conflict resolution.

Like any quest worth its name marriage is sometimes full of betrayal and resentment. The ones we partner with can abandon the quest and we can feel betrayed. When this happens, as with any journey worth taking, it is time to revision the purpose of the journey quest, to get back on track through employing the tactics of forgiveness, accountability and responsibility taking. The question for you to decide is this: is the quest worth taking; is it worth giving your entire effort to? What do you win if you are successful in the quest? Only happiness, meaning and significance and lasting values that you can pass on as a legacy to your friends and children.

Marriage as Conspiracy

Marriage can be viewed as a conspiracy by two people to get their needs met over time and space. It is also a conspiracy and quest for meaning in significance discovered in and through a committed relationship between two people. Why a conspiracy? Consider the etymology of the word "conspire". **Conspiracy** comes from the Latin word 'conspirare' meaning to breathe together. The image is one of a small group of people plotting closely to get something they want, they plot so closely that each person can feel the other's breath. But this meaning doesn't have to be so sinister either, consider your own two lungs. They exist side by side and breathe together, they respire and form, in a sense, a common "breathing together" to help your body get what it needs, air. So perhaps we can truly say that marriage in its simplest form is a close knit conspiracy of a man and a woman to help each other get what they need. They form a bond so intimate that they can feel the hot moist breath of the other, they keep secrets between each other and they form a dyad, just as your two lungs form a dyad to provide oxygen for your body.

An affair is like a conspiracy, but with a bit more sinister meaning and with overtones of betrayal, deceit and deep hurt. We know that people have affairs in part to recover the original feelings of being close to another. A marriage gets stale and a man and woman get stuck in their separate roles, the passion dies, the children grow, communication fails, and before one realizes it there is an affair.

Often, the remedy for an affair, if the damage is not too great and a couple re-chooses their marriage, is to have the couple conspire again to love each other, to become more passionate for each other, to have an affair with themselves. Isn't this what the beginning courtship and falling in love period represents? A couple cling to each other, almost glom to each other so as to exclude others, they can't get enough of each other. Of course, as the marriage progresses, this energy gives way to a more structured way of begin together. Spouses cannot simply stay up until 2 am talking about their love for the rest of a marriage, Passion often gives way to structure and some routine. But a couple who wishes to continue to renew themselves does not want to totally forget the passion and energy that brought them together.

Your Journey Quest, Your Marriage Quest

So the question that each of you needs to answer is whether you agree that your marriage is really a quest, a journey quest that spans time and geography, that involves transition and challenge, a quest where you need to meet challenges with the right tools and weapons and if you don't your own partnership can be threatened and even destroyed. If you agree with this approach then perhaps you are ready to recharge the original conspiracy that the two of you undertook when you decided to join together in love. Perhaps it is time to reenergize that love by looking at where your journey has taken you so far. By reexamining this you may find that your love has cooled a bit, but perhaps you will find that you still have the energy and zest for the challenge, that there is a lot of life yet to live and that the one you are partnered with right now is the one you are choosing to live it with.

When you embark on a journey quest you might ask what tools and companions you will need on the journey. Often, an extended journey will require that you go with someone you trust, perhaps a group of people who can walk the road with you together. Think about who you want to journey with. Your journey will require a strong partnership, companions who can help when the going gets tough, friends who will listen and sometimes challenge, and perhaps someone who you will fall in love with and share the more intimate parts of your journey. This is why the images of friend, companion, partner and lover are the dominant images that help sustain a marriage. In some fashion the person you marry becomes a friend, companion, partner and lover to and for you. You will have other friends and companions, but only one person who you will yearn to call your soul mate, your marital friend and companion. Paying attention to these images will assist you in keeping your relationship true and strong.

Tools for the Quest: Learning to Reflect on Your Life and Relationship

One important tool for any new endeavor that you undertake is that of learning how to reflect on your experience. All of us have numerous and varied experiences, some good, some bad, some happy, some sad. How do we reflect on our experiences so that we can appropriately name what is important and significant about them? Naming has great value and power, for once we name what is going on we can take further ownership of the experience and the process that forms the experience. Naming then leads to greater identity formation and to a deeper formation of the ego. The following steps can help you reflect on your personal and marital experiences.

Awareness

The first step in naming what is happening in your experience is to become aware. But to be aware one must be fully present. It is amazing how often we are not one hundred percent present. Research has shown that children can tell within a few moments when their parents are not present to them. Think of the times when you were a child and one of your parents read to you. You could tell almost immediately when their mind wandered and you called them back to attention to continue reading.

Awareness comes in two basic varieties. We can have conscious awareness where we understand fully what we are about; and then we can have unconscious or semi-conscious awareness where we are only partly aware of what is happening around us. The book "Blink" is based on pre conscious awareness and explores the part of our brain that comes to quick decisions even before we make a conscious decision. This is what we mean by the word "instinct".

The task in this interpretative frame work is to develop the habit of awareness, even of those thoughts, patterns and instincts that lie just below our consciousness. Questions that come from awareness are: Am I acting from any unconscious motives? Can I be aware of what my body is telling me about a particular interaction that I am having? Can I develop a "third eye" about my self in action; can I see myself interacting and become more aware of what my body posture, voice tonality and other mannerisms are communicating? When we embark on developing the habit of being more aware we then become more present to the present moment. We also maximize our ability to be more fully present to relationships.

To summarize, awareness encompasses the following areas:

- My unconscious processes that become available to me on reflection or after an encounter (I blurt out something inappropriate when I'm nervous)

- Feelings and impulses that reside just below the level of my awareness and , like an ice cube, bob up and down in the sea of my awareness.

- What is happening in my body, where I feel joy, sadness, anger, fear.

- Listening to my instincts, my first impulse when a significant event happens or something is said that upsets me or puzzles me.

- The other: becoming aware that other people interpret the same reality differently than I.

- The other: becoming aware of the needs of others and how I might be able to help.

Sometimes, we become aware of a problem; whether it is financial, one involving the kids, work related or interpersonal with our spouse. When this occurs we often want to act right away to solve the problem. Yet there is an intermediate step that needs to be taken.

Discernment

The second step in reflecting on experience is that of making decisions from the awareness that you develop. When you become aware of a problem, or that someone is feeling hurt or angry you have the opportunity to act. But should you? How do you make the decision to act, because intervening sometimes can make the situation worse? Think of a mother and father where a child is giving his mother a hard time. She is getting increasingly upset. The father sees this, is aware of this, then intervenes and disciplines the child, only to have his wife become upset because she didn't ask for the intervention.

When in a serious relationship it usually pays to discern if and how you should act before acting. Discernment of if and how to act implies placing your own awareness in dialog with another person. Using the example above, to say "You're getting upset, do you need help?" is discernment placed in dialog with another. This builds trust and signals you are not trying to take control. Awareness in dialog with another allows each person to bring a problem to the other. Part of the discernment process, however, is that of checking in with another if that person sees the problem in the same way. And because the other is truly the "other" chances are that person will have a slightly different take, or awareness about the problem. Having both of you place your awareness in dialog means that you are open to understanding how the other sees the reality.

Who do we discern with?

- Our spouse, taking that person into confidence, sharing what is going on, how you feel, what is most bothersome or joyful to you

- Our close friends, asking for advice when we become aware of something that presents an obstacle, or a relationship that is causing pain or frustration
- Mentors, when we are confronted with the tough decisions in life, like changing jobs, moving, etc.
- Small communities of intimacy can be scripture or church groups, AA groups, support groups, book clubs; bringing our experiences to such groups in the hopes of gaining support and insight about ourselves and the problems we face.

Action

Once awareness has move to discernment in dialog then the proper action can be taken. Sometimes this action is an intervention directed at the specific problem, sometimes it is a change in behavior on one or both of your parts. For example, suppose your spouse becomes aware that the way you tease causes frustration and some hurt. She brings this to you and asks you to be aware of your behaviors. After talking about it for a while and going through discernment in dialog process you see her point of view. Then it is on to action, where you choose to be aware of your tendency to tease and then check it so that it eventually becomes a past behavior. This is the level of action on your part, a new behavior that arises out of awareness and discernment on the awareness placed in dialog with another.

The dialectic between awareness, discernment and action is a process that you can utilize over and over. It starts with you as an individual, then expands to include your spouse, and expands further to included trusted friends and mentor.

Action is usually best taken in the following areas:

- Ownership of action of the self: I decide to do something different, not give advice to my spouse as to what action should be taken
- The action is specific and is meant to either change the way I perceive things or to change the way I am trying to solve a problem
- The action is meant to proscribe or address a certain behavior of mine that is becoming harmful to me and my relationship. An example is deciding to quit smoking because of harm done to self and others.
- The action is also beneficial to a wider range of relationships, my family, my community, church, work etc. In other words, more than just me benefit by such a change.

Committing to an Ongoing Process, or building Virtue, Not Vice

Once you commit to a process of awareness, discernment and action you begin to embark on a discipline of virtue. Virtue is a good behavior that we do over and over again so that it becomes a good habit. Becoming virtuous is not so that we can be seen as a hero or a nice person; it is so that we can have mastery over those habits and tendencies that dehumanize us, and so that we can assist others to do the same. A vice is a harmful behavior we do over and over again that becomes a bad habit, like over eating, alcohol abuse, smoking, gossip, etc. Harmful behaviors that become habits begin to rob us of our fullest sense of humanity and begin to gradually dehumanize ourselves and others. By committing to the process of awareness, discernment and action you allow yourself to do some self critique, and also self praise, as you understand yourself on a deeper level. Instead of criticizing your spouse you will be reflecting on how you can do better, listen better, and be a better friend and intimate lover for and with your spouse.

A Slice of Life

Tom and Sandra had been married for twenty-four years. They have four children. Their oldest is now a senior in college. The past five years have been particularly tough on them. Their second child, a daughter, became pregnant at age eighteen, had the baby, and then married her boyfriend. And their third daughter struggled all through high school with depression. All these problems caused a great deal of stress in their relationship. Tom found himself withdrawing more and more into his work and avoiding talking over the problems with Sandra. It seemed that every day when he came home he was presented with problems. Sandra felt abandoned by Tom and angry that he had become so avoidant. She felt that he wanted her to deal with the problems and make everything right. At times she would get so angry with him that she would blow up, shout at him and criticize him.

The stress was so intense and their relationship suffered so much that at one point they even talked of separation. At that point they decided to go for marriage counseling. The therapist was able to validate Sandra's anger while encouraging Tom to face the problems more directly. And she encouraged them both to start doing more things for themselves. She pointed out that it had been nearly four years since they actually took time away for themselves. She suggested a "date night" routine where they went out every two weeks just so that they could have time away and check in with each other. At first the progress was slow, but gradually Tom and Sandra began to create more closeness in their relationship. Both are now continuing the routine of regular dates and Tom is more willing to talk about things.

Awareness in Action

- In the above case what are the blocks to deepening the bond in the marriage? Is there a time when a lack of awareness and acting on that awareness has created a bigger problem?

- How do the two of you build in regular check ins with each other that allow you to be aware of the problems you are facing and discern how to address those problems?

- Are there other partners, friends, married couples who shared your common values and vision of the future and help you develop an ongoing discernment about the health and quality of your relationship? Are you still in touch with them, do you still gather with them as companions that share a common experience. Or have your roads diverged? If so, how do you feel about that?

- Are both of you open to discussing the quality and development of your relationship so far? What are the blocks to this happening in a deeper and more satisfying way?

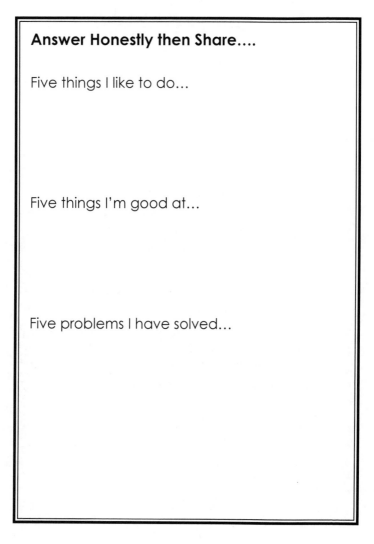

Answer Honestly then Share....

Five things I like to do...

Five things I'm good at...

Five problems I have solved...

2

THE RHYTHM AND NEEDS OF MARRIAGE

Nothing was happening in
my marriage. I nicknamed
our water bed "Lake Placid."

— PHYLLIS DILLER

THE LIFE FORCES AND NEEDS THAT SHAPE YOUR MARRIAGE

Your commitment to each other is founded
on both of you helping the other to meet the
basic needs of life as they unfold throughout
you marriage. These needs arise out of the
basic impulses that shape your lives and which
find expression in your deciding to make a
life together. Two people deciding to commit
to each other respond consciously and
unconsciously to the following forces of life.
At their highest levels these forces give rise to
our deepest yearnings and show themselves
in the formation of a spirituality. Each of these
impulses are expressed individually and come
together

Unitive Force

The Unitive Impulse is what brings a couple together to form a unity of two separate and distinct individuals. This force moves a couple to seek what they hold in common. To be one with the other is one of the most profound experiences a person can have. The unitive force gives rise to the concept of teamwork, people working toward a common goal in life and a general sense of working toward a greater goal. It is expressed best in the phrase, "the two become one". It also gives rise to the search for the transcendent, the search for a higher power that guides all of life. The unitive force gives rise to our quest for God.

Generative/Procreative Force

This Generative/Procreative Force is what impels a couple to attempt to make the world a better place. Generativity is what impels a person to want to make a contribution, to allow the person to go beyond the limits of self gratification to create a different, better world for others. This force often results in a couple's decision to bring new life into the world. The decision to have children is perhaps one of the most traditional ways that a couple enacts this impulse, but there are many other ways that a couple can choose to be generative, from adoption of children in need to deciding to become involved in numerous volunteer activities.

Personal Charismatic Force

All of us have distinct personalities that express themselves in different way. This force addresses the reality that our personal development precedes our marriage commitment and continues throughout the life of our marriage. We have distinct energy levels, distinct talents and traits that allow us to interact with others and which define our uniqueness in the world. The word charismatic refers to the fact that all of us have a unique set of "giftedness", meaning a unique combination of emotional, intellectual and personal characteristics that make us who we are.

In a marriage two people join together to assist the other in the development of this impulse. Career choices and education choices come together here, and personal happiness is often defined through paying attention to this impulse. But there is tension introduced here because it is the responsibility of each person to take responsibility for the expression of this impulse. Sometimes one's personal expression creates tension for and with the other. How assertive you are, what you want out of life, career, how much you can sacrifice for the other, all go into expressing this impulse. Paying attention to this important aspect of being human can help a couple realize that while common interests and values form the basis of a marriage, the personal differences that emerge, and how they are developed, often govern how the marriage will go as the time progresses.

The Rhythm of Marriage

The life forces that shape a person's life is lived out in married life in a continual rhythm that re-cycles throughout the life of a marriage. Like life, marriage has its own rhythm and if we pay attention to that rhythm we can ensure that we are engaged in a continual process of renewal. The rhythm of marriage follows the general pattern of life of *preparation, fulfillment and rest.* We seem to be always preparing for some event, whether it is a holiday or a graduation from college. But life is not only about preparation, it is also about meeting our goal, and when we do this we engage in celebration, we feel fulfilled. And after achieving our goal and celebrating we settle into a routine of applying and living out of our accomplishment. Then, after a time, the pattern recycles when we move on to the next period of preparation as we define the next challenge in our lives.

Marriage follows this general pattern but it has its specific application. In a marriage a couple is always cycling through a rhythm that has the following characteristics: *pursuit, catch/bonding, and rest/routine.*

Pursuit

In this part of the cycle two people begin initially to befriend each other, become attracted to each other and engage in pursuit of each other. When you are courting and falling in love pursuit feels so wonderful, you long to be in the presence of the one to whom you are attracted. It is telling to listen to the attraction stories of a couple, who pursued who, how they did it, who first proposed the idea of marriage and so on. When we pursue each other in the beginning there is a lot of energy.

Catch/Bonding

There comes the time when two people catch each other and begin to bond as a couple, where the bond begins to be expressed more strongly as a commitment. It is at this stage where a couple will announce their engagement and begin planning for the next phase of their lives together. This is an exciting time, but it can also be a time of tension, for some of the energy and hormones of the initial courtship and pursuit will be wearing off. This is also a time when two people, still energized by the first phase, may begin to notice some real differences between the two. This phase culminates in some form of decision to live together and is often followed by a wedding celebration.

Rest/Routine

In this part of the cycle the couple begins to live the reality of every day marriage. Routines are established and if all goes well the couple settles into a comfortable routine. This can be a time of true rest and appreciation of the other, of happiness, but it can also be a time of tension. This is due to the fact that true differences in personality will surface. One spouse might say, "I didn't sign up for this, I didn't know this about you before we were married." Encountering differences can be very anxiety producing but it can also lead the couple into deeper knowledge of self and the other.

Renewing or Stifling the Cycle

Marriages that work find a way to renew the cycle of pursuit, catch and routine, where the passion and energy continues to flow. When this works a couple finds time to pursue each other romantically and emotionally, and reaffirm the original energy of the relationship. This leads to further bonding, and only reinforces the routines established, which in a very important way becomes routines of intimacy and renewal.

But sometimes the relationship hits a snag and instead of renewal of the cycle a knot of tension and conflict is introduced that interrupts the pursuit cycle. Some marriage engage in a downward spiral where instead of closeness there is an increasing level of distance and discomfort. When that occurs the attempts at pursuit degenerate into hurt, argument and more distance. The reasons for these things happening usually rests in one or more conditions being present from the beginning of the courtship:

- One person pursues much more than the other. This occurs when someone tries to get the other person to be more emotional, more outgoing, etc. A pattern gets established where one person expects the other to pursue and doesn't reciprocate. When they are married the one pursuing reaches a point where the pursuit stops.
- Conflict resolution patterns that keep short circuiting the original pattern of pursuit and catch. This becomes a situation of "closeness interruptus", meaning that just as a couple is becoming close, someone gets angry, shuts down or interrupts the completion of the pursuit cycle, thus resulting in both people being frustrated. Once the couple marries, this pattern continues where eventually there is more distance, hurt and anger.
- A harmful or hidden issue that one or both of the spouses didn't see or overlooked. For instance, perhaps a

couple enjoys going to parties with friends, but after the marriage one of the spouses continues to drink. This pattern then begins to be an issue for the other. Another example could be unseen or undiagnosed depression that emerges after the marriage. While not necessarily destructive this type of unseen issue can surely derail the recycling of the pursuit – bonding – routine-ritual rhythm of marriage.

- Unexpected transitions that interrupt the cycle and which place a high amount of stress on one or both spouses. Early marriage is especially vulnerable to these types of transition, be they job loss or change, unexpected pregnancy, illness in one or both spouses or extended family, etc. Transitions that mount up also interrupt the meeting of basic needs, which only increases tension and conflict.

- Unresolved family of origin issues like physical or sexual abuse, alcoholism in the family of origin, etc., all of which cause a person to develop what is known as "maladaptive" defense mechanisms that begin to interfere with the normal cycle of marriage. This type of issue usually requires the help of a trained professional to help with the development of insight and the necessary behavior changes that will be required.

- Unrealistic expectations that lead to anger, withdrawal and increased conflict between the two spouses. Most early marriages face some need to revise expectations and to talk through the disappointment that comes from this. The couple that keeps an open style of communication is best equipped at dealing with this and creating more realistic and life sustaining expectations.

A couple that finds themselves caught in a rut, where the pursuit of each other stops or slows down to the point that both are unhappy, faces a choice: do we try to renew the relationship or let things continue to die? Many marriages are renewed and reinvigorated by a couple making the simple yet profound choice to seek marriage counseling. If this is the case for you, consider getting some help, so that your relationship can be renewed.

Needs in Marriage

The life forces are expressed more specifically in a marriage in each person understanding and helping the other meet the basic needs of life. If marriage is a conspiracy on the part of two people to meet their needs, then what exactly are those needs that most need to be met? The following set of needs is a distillation and compilation of the theories of Erik Erikson, Abraham Maslow and Willam Glasser (Choice Theory), three highly influential developmental theorists of the 20th and 21st centuries. Each theorist has slightly different but also similar characteristics. The combined list of needs can be summarized in the following eight needs:

Safety

- Safety is a core need that precedes all the others, for we cannot communicate, be intimate, learn or have fun if we don't first feel safe.

Love and Belonging

- Another core condition is that of feeling love and belonging in love to a family or group that acknowledges us and cares for us. To be loved, to belong is one of the most powerful forces in the human experience, and without this need being met we can often chase one relationship after another in desperate pursuit of this need.

Power/Competency

- All of us want to thrive, not just exist, we all want to learn new skills, to keep learning and reach our highest potential. Often, fear, criticism and put downs will hold us back and we will feel varying degrees of powerlessness or in-competency.

Respect and Recognition

- Basic respect for the human person is a core need that cuts across all cultures and classes. To be respected is to have your humanity affirmed. To be recognized is to have a voice and feel proud of your talents, your very self.

Creativity/Generativity

- We have an urge to go beyond ourselves through our accomplishments. This shows itself in creative endeavors, art, writing, poetry, invention. Also, this need speaks to the desire to leave the world a better place, and is the need that gives rise to procreating so as to ensure the survival of the human species.

Fun

- When our spirit becomes stifled and we stop having fun, we can feel trapped and that life gives us no energy and passion. Having fun allows us to re-create ourselves and when you put it together allows us to engage in restorative recreation. Fun and recreation are really an offshoot of the need for creativity/generativity but it is helpful to state it as a distinct need, for in practical terms a couple often stops having fun when things become the most difficult for them.

Freedom to Thrive and Change

- To be able to change and develop and to have the freedom to do so speaks to countless generations of people who have been oppressed, enslaved, or harassed by dominant populations. There is a spirit of freedom that cries out against injustice and which impels the person toward creating conditions where freedom reigns.

Transcendence

- We have a basic need to move beyond ourselves, our limits, to recreate ourselves when we are most stressed, most oppressed. This need gives rise to our deepest impulse to be spiritual people, to look for a greater meaning and significance to our lives. It also addresses the crisis of limits, for when we encounter the death of our loved ones, or contemplate our own death, there is something in us that cries out for a greater reality, where all is not just annihilation and final limits.

Marriage represents a life long quest to continually define the needs of each one of you, and to communicate your needs in a way that is both specific and clear. Our behaviors usually flow in the direction of our needs, so if we have a need, for instance, of emotional closeness, we will move in the direction of those people who can meet our needs. While this may appear to be self evident, sometimes we blame the other for not knowing what we need.

A Slice of Life

Carla and Fred have been married for fifteen years. They have three children, ages thirteen, eleven, and eight. Both have worked full time outside the home since their third child began first grade. Up until that time Carla was a stay-at-home mom. Before their first child was born she worked as an accountant for a major health care system in town. She went back to work part time after their second child was born. She really wanted to work full time and was ready to do so, except that she and Fred would argue over her working full time. Fred was adamant that their children have someone at home when the kids came home from school. Carla agreed with this goal, except that she felt that Fred could adjust his sales schedule so that he could be home late in the afternoon. Right when she thought they came to some agreement where she thought she could expand her work hours something seemed to come up with Fred's work schedule that prevented him from following through with the plan.

It wasn't until their youngest began the first grade that Carla insisted on going back to work full time. This created a good amount of tension in the marriage and both Carla and Fred felt at times that the other was giving ultimatums. Both had hurt feelings over the matter and both believed that each of them were the "losers" of an extended power struggle. And while they both believed in their marriage and worked on their relationship together, the topic of careers and work was a sensitive one because of the way the decision for Carla to work full time was made.

Awareness in Action

- Does this slice of life evoke any similar struggles in your own relationship?
- Have there been times in your relationship where the two of you have become competitive about certain issues or needs that you had?
- Have each of you ever competed with the other to get basic needs met?

- When you're stressed and tired is it more difficult to listen to and help meet the needs of the other?
- Think of the original energy that you had when you first fell in love. What attracted you to your spouse? How did each of you pursue the other when you first courted? Do you remember who was the first to ask the other out? How do each of you now pursue and re-energize your marriage?

Spirituality

"Is there any 'there' there?" This was a question asked by a young man who was grappling with the ultimate questions of life. Is there anything that lies beyond my experience, are the quality and energy of my relationships completely lost when I or someone I love die? These are bleak questions, to be sure, but they speak to humanity's need for transcendence. To be human means to test the boundaries of our experience, to try to strive for something beyond our grasp. This has led humans to pursue things like flight and rocketing into space, it lead Einstien to understand the complexities of the created world, and it is the impulse that gives rise to spirituality. Does your marriage mean anything in the grand scheme of things, is it based on a call from a higher power that cares about you and how you treat each other? These are questions for you to answer. Spirituality does not provide answers, but follows its own basic instinct and utilizes your imagine to peer beyond the veil of death to ponder if human energy and effort has a lasting place. Whether you call your God by name, if you profess that something lies beyond, or that there is a life force greater than you, then you are on the ground of the holy in some fashion. Commit to this spiritual journey, for it can help you and your spouse weather the tough times in marriage.

Answer Honestly then Share....

The five things I do for myself to take care of me are....

I am most afraid of... (betrayal, invasion/ violence, being incompetent.)

I am happiest when...

3

THE QUEST FOR FRIENDSHIP

Love is a fruit in season at
all times.
— MOTHER TERESA

Married couples who have been married for
some time often refer to their spouses as their
best friends. Many of us have best friends from
childhood, best friends from work, or best
friends from some other social setting. But the
friendship that develops between two married
people is a special and unique friendship that
takes in the qualities of all our other friendships
yet goes much deeper. That's why the image
of friendship or soul mates is so important in
marriage.

With the image of friends or soul mates, there
emerges a sense of a deep commonality of
values, ways of thinking and feelings between
the two of you. Couples who are friends know
almost instinctively how the other thinks and
can anticipate the other's needs. There is often
an intense energy that exists on the intuitive
level, the deep bond shared between the
two that can appear almost psychic. Here,

the commonality of feelings and values is what brings the friendship into existence. It's common for friends to share similar feelings about an experience. Empathy for the other also runs deep in this image. Empathy means to have deep feelings for what another is going through, be that a happy or sad occasion. To say that one's spouse is a friend implies that he or she is the first person to be consulted in major decisions or happenings, and even in the every day unfolding of life.

It is curious to note that many marriages are the result of spouses becoming friends first and then, only after a period of courtship, lovers. This is true of marriages where the two people knew each other from high school or perhaps met in college, but didn't date for some time. Sometimes, when romantic love begins to intrude on best friends, there is fear that the friendship will be lost or destroyed by the shift. It is possible, however, to be both lovers and friends.

Many times a marital friendship begins to grow stronger after the early years, with their inevitable transitions and crises, have been endured. This can be true for those marriages where the image of lovers has been stressed in the early part of the marriage. This is not to say that the couple are no longer lovers; rather, as time goes on the commonality of values, feelings, and instincts begins to deepen the bonds of friendship between them. And to some extent the couple even goes beyond the parameters of friendship to a much deeper, almost mystical union that can best be described as soul mates. This is a condition where the couple can almost feel their two identities forming a deep unity, which is best described in the quote from scripture: "The two shall become one."

What Sustains a Friendship?

Friendships are often built on four important foundations, fun or enjoyment centered on common interests, meaning centered on common values, emotional support, and time. All four of these are present in a marriage as in any other friendship. It's just that in a marriage a couple will often share much more deeply and exclusively than with other friendships and will have established rules concerning what knowledge of the other is allowed to be shared with friends and acquaintances. In fact, one of the early transitions that a couple often has to make is to realize that the friendship of marriage exists on almost a sacred level, and that each spouse is called to a deep loyalty to the marital friendship. The early crisis of friendship usually centers on one spouse feeling that the other has been unfaithful or disloyal to the friendship by sharing intimate information with other friends, family members, or coworkers.

In order for a marriage to stay healthy the two of you need to work on maintaining your friendship with one another despite all the pressures of parenting, jobs, extended family, and whatever personal difficulties you may be experiencing. By focusing on the four foundations of friendship you will be able to weather the stresses of early and mid-marriage and will discover that your commitment to each other deepens over time.

Fun or Enjoyment Centered on Common Interests

When was the last time the two of you had any fun? Children, as you well know, require a lot of your time, attention, and energy. This can take a toll on your relationship with each other if you are not careful. When you dated and fell in love you probably did things that were fun and energizing. Now that you have moved into the child rearing years, it's more difficult to continue to do the things that you know you both enjoy. But inevitably, there comes a time when you have to face the fact that your life together is more work and less play; getting back to having regular dates with each other is an intervention you will be glad you made.

What are your common interests? Are the two of you doing the things that you used to do when you courted? Or has the business of family, work, and children's activities taken you away from what previously sustained your relationship?

Meaning Centered on Common Values

Deep friendships are not only fun, they also bestow a sense of purpose and meaning to our lives. This is because they are based on a common set of values which gives the friends opportunity to discuss how they see the world, relationships, and the wider issues affecting their world. Part of your attraction to each other was based on admiring certain values and principles in the other. These meaning generating values can become tarnished and rusty if they are neglected due to the hassles of work, parenting, and other commitments. It's important to nourish your souls by giving yourselves the time to check in and deepen your common values. This can be done through gathering with like-minded friends, involvement in a church or other volunteer group, or by attending talks, plays, or movies which sustain, challenge, and deepen your value system. Whatever you do, the most important thing is that you continue this practice as your marriage grows and matures.

Even though friendships are formed around common values, married couples often neglect to surface these values and talk about them. You know that you are on the level of values when you can tell your spouse what you admired the most about him or her when you first met and fell in love. It's still a good idea to revisit the values that originally united the two of you.

Emotional Support

A good friend is priceless. This is the person to whom we will turn when we are down, have a problem, or are just frustrated with the day's hassles. The challenge of married life is for the two of you to continue to give emotional support to each other, despite all the stresses of your present life. One reason why marriages run into trouble is that the marital friendship has been damaged either by lack of attention, constant and unresolved conflict, or the two spouses getting busy with careers and going their different ways. It's much easier to be there for our spouse in good times. But let the stress and strain of life increase and we experience the tendency of me first: "You care for me first then I'll care for you. If you don't care for me first, then I won't care for you and might even retaliate against you." The best remedy for this kind of thinking is to build in frequent, almost daily times to check in with each other. Some people go for walks, some sit down at the end of the day and have a cup of tea, some sit on the couch together while the kids are doing something else. It doesn't have to be very long, maybe fifteen to twenty minutes, but it will return great dividends in later years because your friendship will have been nourished and fed.

Time

Time is our friend, but time can also be our enemy. It is our friend when we realize that it is not an inexhaustible resource but a precious gift. It becomes our enemy when we think we have plenty of it; that we can always get back to repairing a damaged relationship. Many couples back themselves into serious marital trouble by thinking that time alone will heal all wounds. In fact, only two people facing each other and taking responsibility for their relationship can bring about this type of healing. Just as any close friendship can whither away due to neglect, a marriage can slowly but surely starve because of time not taken to sustain the friendship.

A SLICE OF LIFE

Mary and Mike had just bought a car through an online used car dealership. They had to travel about eighty miles to pick the car up. On their way back Mike drove part of the way. As he was getting tired he decided to pull over and so that Mary could drive. Since they were in a rural part of their state of North Carolina he decide to pull over on one of the exit ramps.

He parked the car on the shoulder of the ramp, got out of the car and walked around the front to take his place in the passenger's seat. Mary walked around the back of the car. As she was walking toward the back of the car she noticed another car exiting onto the ramp. This car looked to her to be very close to the shoulder of the road. She continued to walk around the car and was just beginning to turn to walk toward the front door when she looked up again at the car that was exiting. By now it was almost on top of her and she thought to herself that she was going to be hit. She jumped back towards the shoulder and in an instant the exiting car side swiped their newly purchased car, causing damage all the way down the left side.

Mike, by now getting into the passenger seat, felt the car shake from the impact and immediately thought of his wife, who he thought had been hit by the other car. Shouting, "Mary" he leaped out of the car and ran back to find Mary shaken but not hurt. The other car went some distance, then stopped. A young man got out, dazed and shaken. He had apparently fallen asleep for a brief moment and had lost control of his vehicle.

Both Mary and Mike were shaken badly, realizing that a near tragedy had been averted. Their new car was totaled and they had to rent a car to make it home. They drove home in silence. But they held hands, each thinking of the value of their relationship and friendship with each other the past twenty-three years, and how a fluke accident almost wiped out their relationship. Later, both talked about trying to appreciate their relationship more. They both vowed to try to be more present to each other and to let the daily squabbles run off their backs.

Awareness in Action

We sometimes take our friendships for granted even when our relationships are strong and healthy, as in the case above. Has anything similar ever happened to you, where you became more appreciative of your relationship?

- Do you generally feel that you and your spouse are friends?
- What makes your friendship stronger, what blocks it from achieving its full potential?
- Do you and your spouse have as much fun as you used to?
- Are the two of you engaged in meaningful dialog with each other and in outside activities that give the two of you meaning?
- Can you turn to your spouse for emotional support? What blocks this from happening more frequently? Is time a factor?
- Finally, what can you do to take responsibility for your friendship growing and becoming deeper over time?

The Spiritual Dimension: Friendship

Friendship with God is one of the great yearnings of the human experience. In the Christian Scriptures Jesus paid his disciples the highest compliment by calling them "friends" (Jn 15:15). And in the beginning of the book of Genesis, before they sinned, God had an intimate friendship with Adam and Eve. We find that God moved about the garden on a daily basis, and it seems almost as if Adam and Eve took daily strolls with God, their friend.

The original unity present in the Garden of Eden was shattered, of course, by mistrust and dishonesty. The same dynamic plays out in our marriages today. We build our friendship through honesty, sharing, and trust; we harm and sometimes destroy relationships by dishonesty, deceit, and disrespect of the other.

And of course, all special friendships are tested eventually by some crisis, whether it is a crisis of betrayal, or of just drifting apart. The betrayal can be big or small, but when it first comes it hurts, often very badly. But a friendship doesn't have to stop due to betrayal; sometimes a friendship becomes deeper. This is often a major test for a marriage, and many marriages have survived major hurts to the relationship by the couple doing the hard work of reconciliation.

Lasting friendships are like old, gnarled trees that are shaped by the forces of storms and winds that whip and threaten to topple the tree. But the tree grows and forms over time a tough foundation. The gnarls represent the crises that threatened the tree but which eventually led to its rugged beauty. Even the crises of friendship can make a marriage a place of rugged beauty.

Answer Honestly then Share....

I am most ashamed of…

I believe in…

I am jealous of…

4

THE QUEST FOR A LIFETIME LOVER

We practice safe sex. We
gave up the chandelier a
long time ago.
— KATHY LEE GIFFORD

The image "lovers" is the easiest of the four images of married life to grasp, and is perhaps our culture's dominant image of marriage. The image of lovers is self-evident: two people share love and passion for one another, they seem almost bound like magnets. This image is emotionally charged. We often hear people talk about "falling in love," or "being swept off their feet." Some even talk about being destined for each other in a mystical way. The image of lovers naturally refers to a deep sexual connection. After all, being passionate lovers is one primary way that "two become one."

At its deepest level, there is a spiritual dimension to the image of lovers. It speaks to a sense of call to be together, that somehow the union of the two contributes to the building up of the earth and the human community. The book of Genesis speaks of the union of man and woman by saying: "It is good for the two to be together." Thus there is a spiritual affirmation of a deep and passionate love. As lovers a married couple participates in the divine energy through which God created the world. Through creative energy married lovers can say "our love is so deep and intense that we are no longer just two people, in a mystical way we have become one, a new creation."

There is an energy between lovers, a boldness that asserts that the love between the two almost impels them to take risks together that they might not as individuals. There is a felt uniqueness that is shared between the two which states in so many words: "No one but us enjoys the unity and sense of completeness that we feel." And there is a tremendous amount of energy for the relationship. Everything can seem new, even tasks that were once boring or distasteful can appear to be tolerable or enjoyable.

Living as lovers does not mean that a couple will automatically enjoy passionate sex on a frequent basis. After all, our sexual responses are as much learned over time as they are built into our biology. This is often an unrealistic expectation of many newly married couples. The frequency of sex, what gives each person pleasure, and how to achieve pleasure are often unvoiced expectations of early married life. Perhaps the most important aspect of being lovers is that the two people truly enjoy being in each others' presence, both in bed and out, and that they are committed to keeping their life as lovers strong by being passionate about communication and conflict resolution.

The Many Sides of Sex and Sexuality

Sexuality is one of the most important parts of being human and sexual intercourse in marriage is one of the most sacred and profound ways of expressing the love and unity a couple feels. When two people marry they form such a close bond that over the years they share everything about themselves, including their germs and even their immune systems.

Sometimes the sexual activity of a couple becomes burdened by the pressures of married life: too busy schedules, children with their own needs, the burden of work, and an overall tiredness that prevents spontaneity. In the honeymoon phase of marriage things are easy and sexual intimacy seems to come naturally. When the marriage progresses, however, tension and misunderstanding can creep into the sexual life of a couple.

The sexual life of a couple expresses two main realities of marriage. The first is the unitive reality, where sexual intercourse expresses the unity achieved and felt by the couple. The second is the generative and sometimes procreative function, where sexual expression is intended to conceive and bear children.

Frustration occurs when a couple experiences disunity, tension and conflict when trying to engage in sexual intercourse. Sometimes there are arguments, where one person feels that the other does not want to make love as much; other times there is tension because one person may feel objectified by the other. This may occur when one spouse feels that the other is using sex just to relieve the tension of the day. Sexual interaction is also influenced by our prior experiences in life: what we were taught about sex, our early sexual experiences and whether any sexual abuse occurred are all important factors that influence our sexual encounters. All of this can lead to feelings of rejection, embarrassment , anger and even shame.

Here are some tips to keep in mind when trying to keep the sexual passions burning bright:

- Good and regular communication between a couple is like foreplay. A couple that strives to check in and communicate with each other on a regular basis will feel closer to each other, and this closeness will pay dividends in the sexual encounters of the couple.
- Our sexual response is really an integrated response of mind, body and spirit. It is important to understand where our

minds are, are we stressed, depressed or beset by life's burdens? Do we like our bodies, have we gained weight and therefore feel worse about ourselves? Can we be with our partner and actually like our bodies? Do we strive to develop a spirituality of the body and mind that takes into account how our sexual response is part of the overall generative and creative force of love?

- Communicating what turns us on and what doesn't is very important. Letting our spouse know our own vulnerabilities and hurts will deepen trust when it comes time for sexual intercourse.

- Sexual intercourse needs to be placed in the context of respect, safety, love and honesty. We are at our best when we feel respected, when we are safe and when we are communicating honestly in love concerning what is most vulnerable to us.

- Commit to keeping your body in shape as much as possible. This is difficult, of course due to the many stresses of life. Think about how you were when you first were married, how has your body changed since then? Can you commit to taking better care of your body? You will find energy and positive energy when you do so.

A Slice of Life

Amy and Ron have been married for eleven years. They have three children, ages ten, eight-and-a-half, and six. They would both describe their marriage as strong and both are very committed to one another. But they have struggled with a pattern in their relationship that causes both of them distress. When Ron's schedule becomes very busy his stress rises and he becomes more distant from Amy and the children. Sometimes he will work on the computer for hours without talking to her. At the same time his requests for lovemaking increase. At first Amy is ok with this, hoping that if they make love more frequently then Ron will want to talk with her more. But she feels that just the opposite occurs: Ron stays uncommunicative at the same time his physical approaches increase.

At some point in this process Amy gets quite angry with Ron's distance and they have an argument. Amy's anger is centered on Ron's emotional distance, her anger leads her to withdraw from Ron physically. The tension increases and Ron feels pushed away from Amy. Sometimes the tension ends with a big "blow out" argument that clears the air, but which leaves them both emotionally drained. At other times the tension gradually decreases as each maintains distance from the other.

During the times when there is less tension both of them have tried to understand how to break the pattern. Amy has made it clear to Ron that she finds it difficult to be sexual with him when he is emotionally distant. Ron tells Amy that sometimes he feels she uses his emotional distance as an excuse for not being physically close to him, and that there are many times when he is emotionally present to her and where she is still physically distant from him. When that occurs he feels hurt and sometimes rejected. Both realize that when the pattern plays out each of them experience hurt.

Both of them recognize the various parts of the pattern and would like to change it so that they could avoid the conflict and connect with each other on a more consistent basis. They realize that they both have different reactions to stress and different expectations about sex. Even though they are aware of all of this, they keep getting caught in the same, repeating pattern.

Awareness in Action

Maintaining sexual intimacy is an important part of married life. Your sexual life will most likely reflect the ebb and flow of your marriage. Job stress, young children, a lack of time, a lack of communication, and many other things will affect your ability to connect sexually. Often, just making a commitment to focus on the importance of your relationship is enough to restore a balance to your sexual expression.

- When was the last time that the two of you got away and really enjoyed yourselves emotionally, physically and sexually?
- What is the right mix of the four views of sex for you?
- Has your own view of sex as it pertains to your married life changed through the years? How so?
- What is the one thing you want your spouse to understand about the way the two of you engage in love making?
- What is the one thing you can do to increase the reality of the two of you being lovers for each other?

The Spiritual Dimension: Sexuality and Ecstasy

Our sexuality is a fundamental part of being human, and being human, we realize that sex is not only about biology and reproduction, but it goes far beyond biology to encompass spirituality. When you get in touch with the power of sexuality it can be an enthralling experience. You experience the body as good and discover that intimacy between you and your lover is almost limitless. When the two of you become one through love making you experience what the mystics refer to as ecstasy. You feel transcendent, in touch with the divine presence.

The root of the word ecstasy is from the Greek ekstasis which suggests going out of your present state. We know the word today as meaning being overtaken with joy, astonishment, almost in a trance like state. The great mystics achieved ecstasy, and went out of their normal states, through meditation and prayer. They got in touch with the divine through a focused state of prayer that led them into an ecstatic trance.

In the fullest expression of human sexual love something similar happens. You begin perhaps with seeking your own pleasure, but then move out of that state to pleasure the other. Then, in a deeper union of souls, your identity merges for a moment with the other. You and your spouse really are one community for a brief moment. And if orgasm is a physical experience, the ecstasy you feel goes far beyond the physical pleasure. And for a moment the two of you feel the pleasure and ecstasy of God.

Answer Honestly then Share....

One thing I like about you is...

One thing I like about myself physically is...

The one thing I like about my body is...

5

THE QUEST FOR A PARTNER

Any husband who says, "My
wife and I are completely
equal partners," is talking
about either a law firm or a
hand of bridge.
— BILL COSBY

A partnership is usually associated with financial
and legal institutions where there is a very well
defined contract that describes the duties,
responsibilities and benefits of a person in the
partnership. Marriage is a partnership too in at
least three ways:

- Marriage is an economic and legal
  partnership;
- Marriage is a partnership of roles,
  responsibilities and values;
- Marriage is a partnership of parenting
  and child rearing.

There are many benefits to the partnership,
but problems can arise when couples
don't adequately voice their expectations

concerning how tasks and roles will be divided as circumstances change.

Marriage as an Economic and Legal Partnership

This is an aspect of marriage that is often taken for granted and overlooked until there is trouble in the relationship. We all know instances of bitter divorces when a couple has to split up a partnership which has both legal and financial dimensions. This can be quite painful and gut wrenching. Property settlements, pension plans, child support payments and the like all serve as a reminder that marriage, no matter the extent of happiness present, is an economic and legal partnership.

Of course, there are good reasons why a couple embarks on this sort of partnership in the first place. Facing an uncertain financial future can be a daunting task, and given that two people declare their unending love for one another, marriage can appear as a safe haven which provides them both an opportunity to plan for and to create security into their near and long term future. When you married each other, you agreed "to have and to hold, from this day forward. . . ." What is unsaid but very true is that you also committed to "plan and to implement as best we can our dreams for our future." This is why the economic and legal partnership is brought about in the first place.

MARRIAGE AS A PARTNERSHIP OF ROLES, RESPONSIBILITIES, AND VALUES

When two people marry they bring into the marriage certain expectations about what each person will contribute to the marriage. These expectations are often very much down to earth and concrete and center on things like who will do the laundry, who will balance the checkbook, who puts out the garbage, and so on. Also included in this list is a general expectation of what each person needs from the other when things aren't going so well. For instance, the first time one spouse gets sick with the flu usually brings out unvoiced expectations of the other spouse concerning what the flu-ridden spouse needs at that particular time. Some of us revert to a childlike state, others may become cranky, while still others go into themselves and hibernate until the sickness passes.

It goes without saying that many of our expectations about the roles and responsibilities that our spouse will assume are often unvoiced before the actual wedding date. The reality of how someone actually behaves is only truly appreciated when the moment is upon us. The issue of housework, for instance, may be raised before one is married with both spouses sincerely expressing a desire to pitch in and help out.

What then accounts for the surprise and sometimes shock when one spouse finds him/herself doing the brunt of the household cleaning on Saturday morning? Most likely this occurs because our good intentions sometimes run ahead of our actual behavior, which for many of us exists on the level of habit and routine. Whatever the reason, what we say does not always match what we do.

More importantly, a marriage represents a partnership of values which form the basis of the roles we adopt and the responsibilities we assume. Spouses who share equally in household chores, for instance, do so because of the underlying value of equality. Your attraction for each other began, most likely, not only as a physical attraction but as an attraction to the values that each of you embodied. These values need to be affirmed and celebrated throughout your marriage. It's not hard to lose sight of them in the hustle and bustle of married life.

MARRIAGE AS A PARTNERSHIP OF PARENTING AND CHILD REARING

The transition from being a childless couple to having a child no doubt brought about changes in your marriage. Some couples refer this as BC (before children) and AC (after children) because it seems like the life before and after is so clearly demarcated. Consider some of the before and after changes in the following list.

Before children	After Children
A couple can sleep in on weekends.	A couple is usually up by 6 or 7 a.m.
You are accountable only to each other	You are now accountable to three or more
You could go out with friends for a good time	Now you have to find child care
You can make love whenever you want	Now you have to plan around your child's needs
Blissful sleep through the night	One or both of you are up in the night.
Leisure and fun much more spontaneous	Leisure and fun are much more restricted.
Laundry for two	Laundry for three or more

Perhaps you could make an even longer list! There's no doubt that many things change after the birth of the first child. Even more come with the second and third child! And with these changes often come unexpected ways of responding. For instance a husband might assume that his wife is going to get up in the middle of the night because she is breast feeding their child. The wife, on the other hand, might have the expectation that the husband will help her out by going to get their baby, changing the diaper and then bringing the baby to the wife. If these expectations are not talked about, tension will begin to escalate.

STAYING ON TRACK: DEALING WITH TRANSITIONS

A partnership can fail over time if it is neglected and taken for granted. That is a sad thing, but it doesn't have to happen for the two of you if you commit to keeping your partnership on track. The best way to do this is to be aware that in every major transition you will go through you have to rethink how your partnership is lived. Any transition will cause a shift in your roles, responsibilities, and perhaps even your values. If you let the pace and intensity of the particular transition control you, then you may forget to renew your partnership. This is often what happens in the divorces that occur with "empty nest" couples. A couple, married some twenty to thirty years, watches the last child leave only to realize that their marriage was organized more around the children than the two of them. When did that occur? It happened at no particular time, but gradually as the children grew. The important thing to remember is that if a couple checks in on a regular basis, with each major transition that occurs in the family, then their own partnership will be continually renewed and affirmed.

Transitions come in all shapes and sizes. The first year or so after marriage can be a tough transition, when your expectations begin to adjust to the realities of every day married life. The first child is a major transition, as is a geographic move for a job. Promotions, losing a job, career changes are other major transitions. Children going to kindergarten, middle school, high school and off to college are major transitions. And of course, there are the much tougher transitions like major health problems, the loss of a parent or close friend to death, a miscarriage, or even the death of a child. All of these transitions can cause a couple to lose focus and get off track.

You can stay on track with the partnership of your marriage by remembering to:

- Check in with each other concerning expectations, roles, and responsibilities whenever you go through a major transition.
- Talk about and define further the core values of your relationship so that you understand that these values actually form the basis of your partnership.
- Realize that while much of your partnership will be devoted to child rearing you need to plan for the days when your children will be gone. Take the time now to spend time renewing your relationship. Don't wait until the children are gone.

A Slice of Life

Genny sat in church and quietly cried. She kept her tears to herself, carefully wiping them away with a tissue. If anyone around her noticed her tears they at least respected her need for silence. It had been nine months since her marriage of twenty-eight years to her husband had ended, first in a separation and then in a divorce. She was still at a loss to understand what had happened. Her husband had come to her about a year ago and told her that he wanted a separation. She was able to persuade him to enter marriage counseling with her, but as the counseling progressed she could tell that her husband just wasn't into it. Finally, out of exasperation with him she told him that she didn't want him to keep on coming to counseling just to please her. Shortly after that he stopped the counseling and then filed for divorce.

There had been no affair and no real warning signs to tell her that her marriage was in danger. Looking back on things she could now say that she had noticed that their relationship had cooled down a bit. They both had their own routines: she would go to a weekly bookclub, he to golf on Saturday with his friends. Once a week they went out to eat together and on the weekend usually got together with one of their two children and grandchildren. When their children were in grade school and high school they both split up the duties of attending various school events. When the last child left she noticed a gradual lessening of their own interaction with each other, but attributed this to the business of each of their lives. Their sex life, while not as passionate as it once was, was still ok, or at least she thought it was. And where in the past they would fight more, in recent years they fought less, choosing instead to refrain from "pushing each other's buttons." Looking back she knew there were flaws; she just didn't think the flaws were fatal.

When she pressed her husband to explain what went wrong, the best he could tell her was that they had slowly drifted away until one day he woke up and told himself that he wasn't in love with her anymore. Almost on a daily basis for the first four months she woke and asked herself, "How can this have happened to me?" She could come up with no satisfactory answers. She was adjusting, however slowly, to living alone, still shell-shocked from the events of the past year.

AWARENESS IN ACTION

The above case presents the sadness that can come from a marriage ending in a painful divorce. Yet the reality that marriages sometimes end the way this one did might cause the two of you to ask yourselves some deeper questions. While this is sometimes not an easy task it may be well worth the time it takes to be open to re-imaging your marriage as it moves through time. The benefit is, of course, that you both will be in much greater control of defining and attaining your own happiness.

- Does it make sense to you that the way the two of you handle the major transitions in your marriage is important to your future happiness?
- And that the two of you, in order to renew your marriage, have to re-image how it is you will be friends, lovers, companions, and partners as you weather the many transitions you face?

The Spiritual Dimension: Partnership

God, it seems, wants to partner with humanity in transforming the world into the best possible place where justice and peace are primary values. Christianity as a religion places a high value on the fact that God is made human in the person of Jesus. God doesn't do the work all alone but relies on all of us to do our part. The image of walking with us on our road is a comforting one, for sure.

But one doesn't need to be a Christian in order to resonate with the image of the divine partnering with humanity. This image seems to be embedded in most world religions. And it speaks to the interdependence of all of life on earth, where all species play a part in the makeup of the living planet. Perhaps marriage, when at its best, reflects not only the divine partnering with humanity but also that of the earth partnering with humanity to continually evolve and grow.

Answer Honestly then Share....

The emotion that I'm most afraid of is...

The emotion that I find the most difficult to control is...

Five things I like to do just for myself...

6

The Quest for Companionship

When two people love each
other, they don't look at
each other, they look in the
same direction.
— Ginger Rogers

Companionship is another very important
image for enhancing marriage. The quest for
intimacy drives us to seek out someone who
will be there for us in the good times and in the
bad. A companion is someone who agrees to
share with you, scheme with you, and dream
your future with you. A companion is someone
who seeks to join you in imagining what lies
ahead, someone who will create a special kind
of closeness with you, who will share innermost
longings and secrets.

Most importantly, a companion will share
your sufferings and your troubles. The effect
that love can have on another is amazing.
Your spouse falls in love with you, learns about
your physical and perhaps psychological
shortcomings and still wants to be with you
because he or she loves you for who you

are. Later on in life, if you face an emotional or physical hardship, your spouse is by your side, helping you cope and find solutions, not because you are a victim, but because he or she loves you and wants to embrace your troubles. A companion in marriage is the human face of God walking your walk and talking your talk, even though the walk and the talk are sometimes very troubled.

We all walk the road of life. Many times we want someone to be there for and with us. This is what marriage is all about. When a couple marry they know implicitly that they will encounter unknown surprises, both good and bad. The image of companionship reminds the couple that wherever the road goes each person does not have to walk it alone.

Life is seldom a straight and even road. It comes with all kinds of bumps and twists. We can be hurt, sometimes very deeply. We look to our spouse to help us when the messiness of life becomes too much. A crisis seems to be always just around the corner, and with it comes the fear. Will we be faithful to our chosen path? Will we continue to be companions for one another despite the messiness of our lives? What if the road becomes cluttered with obstacles and the going gets tough?

To really share a life together with someone, to be a companion, means that we will get our hands dirty. Everyone's life story has both accomplishments and leftover hurts. Now that the energy of early love has faded a bit we understand more deeply the good and the not-so-good in the person we married. The power of companionship comes from the act of expressing one's fidelity to the messiness of commitment to another. To be able to say that we will be faithful even though the future is unknown takes a certain amount of courage and trust. Whatever problems emerge we pledge ourselves to somehow find solutions.

This ideal of companionship means that as your relationship matures, you must accept each other's personality quirks and foibles. That is part of your commitment. It also means that sometimes you must confront together more serious issues that were hidden at the beginning of your marriage. For instance, a spouse confronting a drinking problem and making the choice to go into recovery is just one way that the unfinished business of life intrudes into the space of the marriage. Or perhaps some ten years into a marriage, a person begins to realize that he or she must deal with the effects of a verbally abusive family of origin. Issues like these are certainly "messy," and there is often a good deal of unresolved anger and resentment experienced. There can also be some dysfunctional behavior on the part of one or both of the spouses.

To commit to finding a way, to working out a process of recovery and reconciliation in the midst of painful discoveries or hurtful behavior patterns is part of companionship. To be a companion with someone who is hurting is perhaps one of the most significant ways we can love someone. That is why the image of companionship begins to take on more significance as a couple endures times of significant change, whether it is the change of having the first child or simply a change in jobs that requires a move to a new city.

Being companions can also create energy. In times of joy and accomplishment, the job promotion, pregnancy, graduation from college or grad school—and many others—provide us opportunities to be there and celebrate with our spouses. Celebrating the good times is all the more important when we recognize that we have been together in the bad times.

While we all appreciate companionship, there are at least two challenges we must confront: the lack of time and the failure to make companionship a top priority. Time is easy to understand as a threat. Sometimes we get so busy with our work or family activities that we simply forget to show up and be there with our spouse. The first time this happens we can be easily forgiven. The second time, not as quickly. By the third time we're beginning to form a pattern of neglect which can be deadly to the relationship. This leads into the second danger: not making companionship a top priority. When the crisis occurs this is what we will hear from our spouse: "You're never around, you're always busy doing other things. I wonder if you love me."

The remedy: make time to be a companion, discover what's blocking you from getting closer, be honest, talk it through. Declare your love for one another, even though it's not easy and get help if you need it. Believe that your relationship with one another is truly unique and thus worth working on and saving. Trust in God, role up your sleeves and get your hands dirty with the messiness of your love for one another and commitment to each other.

A Slice of Life

Pam and Terry have just been through the marital equivalent of a major earthquake, yet somehow their marriage has survived. Terry just recently has entered recovery and now openly admits that he has a drinking problem. He now describes himself as a "recovering alcoholic." Just two years ago he resisted the thought that he even had a problem with drinking. Both can remember the screaming matches they had over Terry's drinking, and how their three children would often place themselves in the middle of the fights just to interrupt them.

One day Pam said very clearly to Terry, "I love you and want to be your life's companion. But you have to decide whether you love me or your drinking. It can't be both." Terry had made several previous attempts to control his drinking. He had even entered an intensive outpatient recovery program. But each time he gradually resumed his drinking.

This time, however, was different. He sensed an urgency to Pam's statement and knew that he might lose his marriage. He returned to Alcoholics Anonymous and began in earnest his recovery. He stated to Pam that he didn't want his marriage to break up. Pam didn't want the marriage to end either; she was hopeful that Terry's drinking days were over.

Now that Terry is moving into recovery they both realize that there is much damage to their relationship that needs to be repaired: trust that was broken, threats that were made, and even Pam's fear that Terry might one day resume drinking are just a few of their present issues. Both were scared about repairing the damage yet both stated that they had been through too much to call it quits now. So they tell themselves that somehow they will finish the project of their marriage that they began some fifteen years ago.

Awareness in Action

Sometimes we don't feel that our spouse is "there for us." Sometimes we have to take the risk of asking him/her to work with us to be a more complete companion. We have to acknowledge that sometimes there are hurts and fears that keep us from experiencing a deeper companionship with our spouse. We may have to realize that we have unrealistic expectations. We might have to challenge ourselves to be a more complete companion. The mirror of marriage has two faces.

- Have there been times when you really came through for your spouse in times of pain or sorrow?
- Were there times when your spouse was present to your own pain and sorrow?
- Are there real hurts that prevent the two of you from becoming deeper companions in the journey of life? What are they?
- How can you move beyond them to a deeper reality of marriage?
- In the above slice of life alcohol abuse as part of Pam and Terry's "messiness." What defines the "messiness" of your life situation that, if worked on could bring the two of you together?

THE SPIRITUAL DIMENSION: GOD AS THE UNSEEN COMPANION

When the going gets tough we often look to be rescued, and when truly bad things happen to us—like illness or the death of a loved one—we often feel abandoned by God. Why do innocent people suffer, sometimes greatly?

God does not rescue us from bad situations, but can turn those bad situations into moments of revelation to us. Instead of God as rescuer think of God as a companion who walks with you in the good times as well as bad. A companion doesn't take away your pain as much as be present to your pain. And in the being present the pain—along with the person—is often transformed. Maybe that is how God works in our lives.

There is a story in the Gospel of Luke about the disciples on the road to Emmaus shortly after Jesus was put to death by crucifixion. They were grief stricken and scared. Unknown to the two of them Jesus begins to walk with them as a stranger. He is present to their pain, to their own agony. And as they walk he helps them interpret their experiences so that they finally recognize him as their friend (Lk 24:13-35).

In a way God walks with us as the hidden companion, not taking away our pain, but being present to us, helping us interpret all the many experiences that sometimes just don't make sense.

Answer Honestly then Share....

The most difficult thing I have ever done is....

In an argument with someone I love I fear most....

When I argue I usually feel...

7

COMMUNICATING EFFECTIVELY

*I can't get along with my
wife—she understands me.*
—HENNY YOUNGMAN

If communicating effectively was all that easy then there wouldn't be an entire industry devoted to helping people communicate in the workplace and home. Perhaps the two biggest areas needing improvement that couples consistently cite have to do with the quality of communication that exists in the relationship and the way that spouses solve their conflicts. In the final analysis, good communication between spouses paves the way for effective conflict resolution.

We learn how to communicate from our own families and from the friends we get to know growing up. The family is the first learning laboratory for a lot of interpersonal skills that we will later take to our adult relationships. But there is another layer of influence that we need to pay attention to: culture. It has a pervasive influence on how our communications are shaped.

Deborah Tannen, the author of You Just Don't Understand (Ballantine Books, New York, 1990), makes the point that in our culture men and women have been taught or "inculturated" to view information from two very different perspectives. And information about one's life, from the day-to-day goings on to the emotional states we might be experiencing, is the life-blood of the marriage relationship. Tannen suggests that women generally use information to build rapport with others while men generally view information as something to report about to someone higher up in the work hierarchy. Men, according to this view, will be more willing to give crucial information to their boss and less willing to give information to their peers.

This is why, according to Tannen, there is sometimes tension at the end of the day when husbands and wives try to talk. The wife, who sees information as something to be shared with those she trusts, even down to the details, asks, "How was your day?" But instead of being met with a full, detailed description, she is only given an abbreviated "bulleted" list of events by her husband. "I got to work, we had a meeting, I had lunch with Joe, then I made of bunch of phone calls to my clients." This exchange leads to the oft-repeated remark, "He doesn't communicate with me." What the woman is actually saying is, "I want to hear more about his day, what happened, and how he feels."

Part of the above dynamic, if it operates in your relationship, might have to do with the fact that the husband is unconsciously hearing a request of a superior when asked for information. Of course, we consciously know that our spouse is not our boss, but sometimes we react on the unconscious level to these legitimate requests for information. Both spouses need to keep in mind that each person brings to the discussion different approaches to communication. Husbands need to look carefully at whether information sharing is really organized in a hierarchal manner in their worlds. In other words, do you flinch when your wife asks you for information, and if you do, is it because you really don't want to "report to your wife"? Once you can identify this you can talk about it and move beyond this negative dynamic.

Another important thing to remember is just how complex communication between two people really is. We often forget this and assume that communicating is something done rather easily. Take some time and look at how most communications happen. The process explains why even simple communications between spouses escalate into arguments.

The Process of Communication

1. Sender: The one who communicates a message:

- Communicates at between 100 and 120 words per minute.
- Sender's communications influenced by:
  a. beliefs about how the world works and how people act,
  b. attitudes toward the future and one's expectations for an outcome,
  c. generalizations and assumptions about people's behaviors and their motives,
  d. stereotypes: rigid generalizations attached to a specific group of people.

2. Sender Communicates Meaning Through:

- verbal content: what is actually said,
- body posture: facial expressions and body position that communicate a feeling message (I'm angry, tense, excited, happy, etc.),
- voice tone: voice tonality also communicates feelings of happiness, anger, frustration, sadness, etc.

3. Listener: The one who receives the message and interprets meaning:

- Picks up on only 7% of a message communicated through actual verbal content.

- Gives special importance to how the message is communicated through body posture and voice tonality.
- The listener's inner self-talk happens at a rate of 600 words per minute compared to the sender's rate of speech of around 100 words per minute.
- The listener filters what is heard through his or her beliefs and themes about himself or herself and the sender. These beliefs and themes have to do with unresolved meta-issues like inclusion/exclusion, dominance/submission, power/powerlessness, belonging/rejection, respect/disrespect. This is why the listener pays special attention to voice tonality and body posture.

4. Tendency for the Listener to React Before the Sender Is Finished Speaking.

- The listener has an immediate feeling reaction about what he or she is hearing based on how he or she interprets the sender's communication.
- The listener tends to listen to the initial parts of the sender's communications before his or her own inner self talk takes over.
- The listener tends to read the sender's mind, thinking that he or she knows what the sender is saying before it is actually said.

- If there are any unresolved "meta-issues" in the listener's life there is an increased tendency for these to become "hot buttons" that the listener allows to be pushed.
- The listener quickly becomes a sender. The sender quickly becomes a listener. There is a built in tendency for miscommunication and arguments to develop.

Sending and Listening

The process above breaks down communication into a sending and receiving part. In reality, when we communicate we oscillate rapidly between being a sender and receiver. That's why it's so hard to really communicate and listen to the other person. Not only that, but the way we communicate is influenced by so many things, like our beliefs about the world and other people. Add to that the fact that we don't really communicate with just words, but with our entire bodies, and you can begin to see that there is a lot going on in a communication. Couples who have a lot of tension in their relationship will tell you that they often communicate better with one another and actually listen to the other when they talk on the phone. Why is this so? Because a phone conversation filters out one of the major ways we communicate, that of body posture, which includes dirty looks, frowns, and the like.

Inner Self-talk

Another thing that goes on in a communication is that we know that the sender communicates at around a 100 to 120 words-per-minute rate. But if you're the listener, your own inner self-talk is zipping by at around 600 words per minute. And that inner self-talk has to do with responding immediately to the first words out of the other's mouth. In other words, you forget to listen to the whole communication and start responding. If you're a man, there is a higher probability that you will interrupt your spouse before she is finished speaking. This is because of the rapid rate of your internal dialog.

The Meta-issues

Another thing that makes communication really tough is that we all carry around in us deeper issues and messages about ourselves, what we will call meta-issues. These are the left over themes from our childhood that never quite got resolved. They are the larger, deeper identity issues that define what gives us meaning and also what we fear the most. Themes like, inclusion/exclusion (am I in or out?), dominance/submission (am I on top or on the bottom?), power/powerlessness (do I have power and competence or am I powerless?) and safety/insecurity (am I safe or in trouble?). Meta-issues have to do with arguments that get started that really aren't about the superficial content, but often point to deeper issues in the relationship.

These meta-issues are questions we bring to any conflictual situation and they represent our worst fears about the future of our relationships. Not all of us have the same deeper issues. It's up to you to figure out which deeper meta-issues shape your agenda of listening. When we have conflict with someone we listen at an unconscious level to hear if the other person is seeking to attack us where our worst fears reside. So, if I fear exclusion, I will listen to see if any of your language about me seems exclusive. And if I perceive you're trying to exclude me then my fear will start to rise and I will respond by trying to protect myself. When I do that I will flip quickly to become a sender and attack your meta-issues, without meaning to of course. And thus the conflict begins to escalate, some times quite rapidly.

Steps Toward Effective Communication

So how do we really communicate with another, and really listen to our spouses? The following five steps are meant to help you begin the process.

1. Drive out distractions:

When listening, focus your attention on the sender. Turn off the TV or radio. Look at the person in the eye and give him or her the benefit of your care and attention.

2. Turn down your inner self-talk:

Imagine that there is a dial on you from 0 to 10. At 10 your inner self-talk is going at 600 wpm. Can you turn down the dial so that you reach a level of around 200 wpm or less? If you can, you'll be surprised at how well you will be able to listen.

3. Make the unconscious conscious:

This is true for any of the deeper meta-issues which affect you right now. Talk to your spouse about them. Let him or her know that sometimes some of your deeper fears get touched when you communicate with one another. Chances are your spouse is not meaning to touch these fears and will be aware of them next time around.

4. Check things out, don't assume, don't think you can mind read:

Check out assumptions. Ask the other if a scowl, for instance, really means that he or she is angry with you. Don't interpret another's non verbal communication and act. Check it out first.

5. Place your emphasis on listening:

We all want to be heard and find our voice. But if everyone talks first then there will be no one to listen. Practice the art and gift of listening with your spouse.

A Slice of Life

Carolyn and George had been married for three years and they recently had a baby girl. Carolyn had decided to take maternity leave from her work for three months. She hadn't yet decided whether she would return on a full or part-time basis. At first she enjoyed the time at home with their new baby. But then, as the weeks went by, she began to miss the companionship and stimulation that she got from being at her work. She also began to depend more on George for emotional stimulation and nurturing.

George was going through some tough transitions at work and his own stress level was rising. He tried to be present to Carolyn when he came home from work and felt that he did a pretty good job of listening. But there were times when Carolyn felt that George didn't really want to hear about how her day went and she felt a bit discounted now that she had the unglamorous job of childcare. She sometimes noticed that George's attention would drift when she would tell him about her day. When this occurred she felt ignored and excluded.

She would get angry with George when he got distracted. George felt that he was in a no-win situation, that try as he might he couldn't meet Carolyn's need to talk with him.

After about three months of struggling with the issue of being present to one another things started to get a bit better. Carolyn was able to return to work on a part-time basis, which gave her an opportunity for adult conversation with others. She became aware of how difficult it was to rely on George for "adult" contact. She also became aware of how difficult the transition to parenting had been on her. She also became aware that she was both afraid and angry that George wouldn't love her as much because she gave up an influential job to stay home with their baby. She realized this was her own fear of inadequacy, but she still felt vulnerable in talking to George about this issue. But they both made the commitment to talk things through no matter whether feelings were hurt. Both valued their friendship with one another and wanted to keep things on track.

Awareness in Action

The above scenario presents a deeper meta-issue in Carolyn's life—that of being ignored and excluded—that affected her relationship with her spouse.

- Are there similar deeper issues in each of your lives that sometimes affect the way you communicate with each other? Can you name them?

- What is the most difficult part of being a receiver/listener for you?
- What can you do differently and better to improve the way you listen to your spouse?

The Spiritual Dimension: Communication

One of the most important characteristics that sets humanity apart from the rest of the created world is the development of language. Certainly, other species have developed methods of communicating between themselves: birds sing, wolves howl and prairie dogs thump with their tails. All of these are forms of communication, but we humans have made communication a sophisticated art form, from cave walls, to billboards, to books and now computers.

Teilhard de Chardin, a great scientist-theologian of the twentieth century, held that love was the language of the universe. There are other scientists that speak of the universe as one large information system which seeks ever increasing levels of complexity. But suppose de Chardin is on to something, that somehow the energy that is love actually created the universe and now seeks to communicate and express itself not only through matter, but through the human community. This is what the Gospel of John is suggesting in its opening words, "In the beginning was the word. . . ." It's all about communication, about information, but most importantly about the communication of love. Do our own words build a world where love is present?

Answer Honestly then Share....

Right now I am feeling.....

I will take responsibility for my feelings by....
(describe the behavior you will do).

The thing that gets me the angriest and most
upset is...

8

COMMUNICATING INTIMACY

Keep your eyes wide open
before marriage, half shut
afterwards.
– BENJAMIN FRANKLIN

It's a "no brainer" that intimacy is an important ingredient in making marriage work. Study after study confirms that both men and women list intimacy as a key factor in marital happiness. But here's the problem that married couples face: if everyone knows that intimacy is such an important thing in a marriage why is it so difficult to obtain? That's the million-dollar question.

Lets start with an image: suppose we say that intimacy is the water that floats the boat of your marriage. Developing the image we can say that marriage is like taking a canoe trip together down a river. The surrounding shoreline serves as the context of your marriage. As you drift or paddle by you sometimes observe a quiet pastoral setting with tree lined shores and a calm easy flowing river. Life is good. You and your spouse, in your canoe, move almost effortlessly down the river. Every once in a while you pull into shore for a break, get the picnic basket out and have some food and drink. You're so relaxed that you might even make love on a secluded beach.

But life moves on. You get back into your canoe and shove off, happy to be together. The water—in this case intimacy—is deep enough to float your boat, and its currents take you along almost without any effort. Then, things begin to change. They can change gradually or suddenly, but eventually your canoe enters rough water and both of you get more concerned about keeping your boat from getting swamped. Suddenly you realize that this canoe trip—intimacy—isn't as fun as it used to be; in fact, it can be a plain bother. Not only that, but now the two of you are shouting directions at each other, often at cross purposes. You even resort to saying things like, "That was a stupid move," and, "I can't believe you did that." Both of you become angry and hurt.

You survive the rapids and learn a few things about keeping your canoe afloat in rough water, but both of you are a little bit hurt and angry at the other for the sharp words. You drift silently for a while pondering what to do and say. Suddenly your canoe runs aground; you have reached a shallow part of the river where there is only about three inches of water and you have to get out and pull the canoe forward. You pull and pull but the water doesn't get any deeper. Again you start to argue with each other. "We should have gone down that other fork. I can't believe you wanted us to take this one." You argue about your direction, compete for control, and realize that you can't really go back. All you can do is go forward and hope the water eventually gets deeper. You begin to say to yourself, "This trip isn't as fun as I thought it would be."

Intimacy, like water, comes in all forms. Sometimes it comes to us as gentle water, soothing and sustaining. Sometimes it comes as a rainstorm, where there are problems to be faced and issues to discuss. And sometimes it feels like the intensity of a hurricane, where all you can do is try to keep your balance and take shelter. And while we all say we want intimacy in a relationship, what we really mean is that we only want the gentle sustaining intimacy where we have good feelings and low conflict. What we don't bargain for is the intimacy of honest conversation where anger and conflict are directly faced. And more than that, sometimes the intimacy seems to go away completely and we're left to pull the boat of our marriage by ourselves, not feeling very in love with the person who agreed to take the journey with us. When we encounter the scary side of intimacy, many of us want to run and avoid.

Another difficulty with the word intimacy is that men and women mean slightly different things when we use it. Intimacy is often defined as affection, fondness, love, tenderness, experience, familiarity, understanding, closeness, friendship, coitus, intercourse, love making. That's quite a list and covers a lot of territory. There are certain subtle nuances to the word that it's important to understand if we really want to communicate with each other in a way that is intimate. According to one study there are at least five nuances to the word intimacy that affect a married couple (Gold, J.M., "Gender and Intimacy," The Family Journal, 5(3), 1998, 199-203). They are:

1. Emotional intimacy as closeness and sharing of feelings. This includes all the feelings, especially anger. In this definition closeness comes from the sharing of feelings.
2. Social intimacy as sharing friends and social networks. This type of intimacy places emphasis on getting together with friends and associates, whether the activities be playing cards, partying, tailgating, or just a quiet evening of conversation.
3. Intellectual intimacy as sharing of ideas and values. Does it surprise you that this

type of sharing creates intimacy? Think about it. Weren't there times in college or high school where ideas really turned you on and you were attracted to people because of the ideas and values they talked about? That's what we're talking about.

4. Sexual intimacy as sexual expression and passion. No need to expand here. This is a very obvious aspect of intimacy.

5. Recreational intimacy as playing and having fun together. "Are we having fun yet?" Well, are you? Marriage should be a source of fun for two people. "But how can we have fun when we're sharing conflictual feelings and even anger?" Intimacy really is more complicated than we realize.

When researchers look into the difference between men and women on the topic of intimacy they come up with some interesting findings. Women tend to place a higher emphasis on understanding and acceptance, trust and commitment, caring and support, and the sharing of feelings. No surprise here. Men place higher emphasis on maintaining good feelings and harmony between the two. What this means is that when a woman wants to talk about something conflictual the first instinct of the man might be to downplay the conflict. The man means well because he is acting out of his understanding of intimacy. But the woman will often take the downplaying as avoidance and become either more angry or more hurt. Complicated business, intimacy.

Wives indicate more dissatisfaction with the emotional and intellectual aspects of marital intimacy whereas husbands report greater dissatisfaction with the social and recreational components.

What this means is that there is a tendency for wives, when dissatisfied, to feel cut off emotionally and intellectually from their husbands. They might complain to a friend that their husbands don't share their feelings and don't communicate with them as much as they would like concerning their thoughts on current events, their values, the issues at the job site, and the like.

Husbands, when dissatisfied, tend to feel that their wives do not want to participate with them as much in social activities or in social networks; they also may feel more cut off from their wives in terms of doing things together recreationally. Also important for husbands is the maintaining of harmony in the relationship.

Here, it is important to note the distinction between having "good feelings" or harmony and the sharing of feelings. While women place more emphasis on the sharing of feelings, men often get themselves into a bind when they begin to think that the sharing of what they perceive as "negative" feelings (anger, hurt, sorrow, etc.) will destroy the harmony in the relationship. If husbands could understand that the expressing and talking about "negative" feelings will build harmony between the two then they might be more willing to partake in an exchange of feelings with their wives.

What about sexual lovemaking? Recent studies indicate that this aspect of intimacy is valued just about equally between the sexes as an important part of intimacy. This may come as a surprise to some readers, due to the stereotype that suggests husbands wanting to make love more than their wives. However, there seems to be more equality between husbands and wives concerning the importance of lovemaking in the relationship. At least one researcher claims that couples who maintain a frequency of lovemaking at least once a week report a higher marital satisfaction.

BLOCKS TO INTIMACY

Clearly, there are times when we cannot communicate what we want. You love each other yet find there are times when instead of communicating love, tension and conflict result. John Gottman, author and marriage researcher, cites four potentially dangerous communication patterns that will eventually kill a marriage. In his book **Why Marriages Succeed or Fail** he calls these patterns the "Four Horseman of the Apocalypse" for marriages, because their presence will truly erode the grace and goodness of the marriage. The four horsemen are:

Criticism	Attacking the position of the other by making his or her position or behavior appear wrong	Use of "never" and "always" in dispute, use of blaming of the other for something that went wrong.
Contempt	Attacking the person of the other by use of hurtful and negative personal characteristics.	Use of name calling, "you're stupid", hostile humor or sarcasm, use of words like, "bitch, bastard, witch, ugly, lazy, fat, etc".
Defensiveness	Seeing the self as a victim of an attack, attempting to ward off the attack	Making excuses, invoking "it's not fair", using the defenses of rationalization, intellectualization or denial to ward off perceived attack.
Stonewalling	Withdrawing from conflict "shutting down, shutting up".	When problems or issues are brought up, or when feelings are hurt, the person withdraws and becomes silent, just not dealing with the issue or person.

The presence of these destructive communication patterns is similar to taking a small amount of herbicide and every day putting some of it around your favorite tree. One small dose of the herbicide might not kill the tree outright, but a continual application will eventually begin to undermine the root system of the tree, resulting in eventual death of the tree. Your relationship is like a tree that needs to be protected from toxic communication patterns. Make a commitment to root out these patterns so that each of you can maximize the potential of your relationship.

A Slice of Life

Carol was twenty when her parents divorced. At the time she was a sophomore in college and she took the news quite hard. She knew that her parents had argued frequently but always assumed that they would "kiss and make up." She simply had no clue that their marriage was in trouble.

The explanation both of her parents gave her was the same: there had been no affairs and both had simply drifted apart from each other over the years. Her dad would golf regularly while her mom played tennis and had an active social life outside the home. She just never saw any of this coming.

The next few years were tough on Carol. She finished college but her grades suffered a bit. Her own sense of self-trust and self-esteem, which hadn't been all that great before her parents' divorce, now began to suffer even more. She experienced a number of quick, intense relationships with men, all of them ending abruptly and all of them causing her concern about her ability to enter into a long term relationship.

Now at age thirty-one Carol was facing her first crisis in her own marriage. She and Matt had been married for eight years and had two young children, ages five and two. Carol was beginning to feel that she didn't love Matt anymore. Their courtship had been one where Matt had been the primary pursuer. Carol had been reluctant at first and had rebuffed Matt's advances on a number of occasions. But Matt had been determined and they eventually began to date. Carol found Matt to be sensitive, caring, and organized, but conservative in his tastes and habits. While Carol liked to go out dancing or be with friends, Matt preferred a quiet evening at home. And when she would express her dissatisfaction she felt that Matt was dismissive of her point of view. It was almost as if he didn't want to talk with her, which was confusing. In the early years of courtship and marriage they had often gone for long walks and Matt seemed intensely interested in her thoughts and feelings.

The way Carol put it, there was little "pizzazz" left in the relationship. She began to wonder if she had made a mistake in marrying Matt and whether he appeared a "safe" bet to her, coming off of the turmoil created from her own parents' divorce. She knew that she was also a bit overwhelmed from being a mother of two young children and wondered if she just wasn't burned out altogether. She recently had begun losing weight and began waking up around three in the morning. All she would do was worry. She wanted to take the risk and tell her husband how she felt, but was afraid that he would dismiss her concerns again. Yet she knew that she was becoming increasingly dissatisfied.

AWARENESS IN ACTION

It's easy to be completely present to someone when you're not hurried, stretched, or stressed out from the daily rhythm of life. Marriage is sometimes like a juggling act: we try to keep all the objects in the air, in balance, not dropping anything. It takes practice and discipline to live a busy, stressed existence and take time to listen to the ones we love. We need to remember that we juggle all the things of married life because they are worth keeping in the air, worth not being dropped. Maybe we need to think about being more appreciative of the things that our spouse keeps going and communicate that to him/her. At the same time we sometimes get out of touch with what first attracted us to each other.

- Are the descriptions of the ways that men and women understand the word intimacy true of you and your spouse?
- Are anger and dealing with hurt feelings the scariest part of intimacy for you? If so, what makes this either scary or difficult?
- In the above slice of life Carol was afraid to talk to Matt about her feeling that their marriage had cooled off. What prevents you from dealing with the tougher issues? Do you fear rejection?
- What is the benefit of taking the risk to deal with the tough issues?
- Finally, is there anything that you want to do differently in order to take responsibility for how you create intimacy with your spouse?

THE SPIRITUAL DIMENSION: INTIMACY AND SPIRITUALITY

"If God were one of us, just a stranger on the bus . . ." goes a popular song. But suppose God really was one of us. Would God need to share feelings, values, and have fun together with friends?

And most important, would God be open to suffering, to getting old, to having people disappoint and not keep their word? Christianity as a religion is based on that very premise: that God is a stranger on the bus. Except that Christianity holds that God is not a stranger, but is revealed to us in the stranger, as well as in those we know and in our spouse.

What if each of us carries within us the "God-force," what we traditionally have called the Spirit of God? If we took this seriously would this change the way we communicated with each other? Perhaps we would value just a little deeper the intimacy that we created, knowing that it partakes in the mystery which we name as God and creator.

Answer Honestly then Share....

When I get angry I need....

If I had a magic wand and could use it on my intimate relationship(s) I would change...

What pleases me most about my skills are....

9

KNOWING YOUR APPROACH TO CONFLICT

I suspect that in every good
marriage there are times
when love seems to fail.
—**MADELEINE L'ENGLE**

The successful resolution of conflict is so important in a marriage. That is why it is important for spouses to understand .how each of them enters into and resolves conflict. Each of us has a definite style in the way we approach conflict and what we do when conflict begins.

Each of us has two reactions or approaches to conflict. The first approach is our initial instinctual response, where we follow the roles and patterns that we have integrated into our personality. The second reaction or approach is how we react once conflict has escalated to a "decision point." This "decision point" is like a fork in the road. One fork takes the couple down the road where conflict continues to escalate in unhealthy ways. The other fork leads to attempts to de-escalate the conflict by building bridges and problem solving.

Our Instinctual Response

In the previous chapter you read about the importance of problem solving as well as the larger meta-issues that sometimes prevent you from solving your problems. These are issues that are usually rooted in our own families of origin. Another thing we have learned from our families of origin is our response to conflict. We continue to use this approach because it has been, to some extent, helpful to us in negotiating conflict.

The following represent four major styles that we bring into any initial conflict.

1. Pleaser-Soother

The pleaser-soother, when faced with the initial conflict, will immediately try to make his or her spouse happy. This person's main objective is to calm down irritated feelings and try to please the other by either being agreeable or stating such things as "it's not that bad." In this person's world there is a belief that conflict is dangerous and that it can only lead to worse things happening. Further, this person believes that harmony, above all else, is the most important thing in a relationship.

This style of approach can anger the other spouse because he or she might feel that the initial approach of soothing and pleasing is in fact avoiding the problem. If you're married to a pleaser-soother try to realize that your spouse is not necessarily trying to avoid the problem as much as minimize its emotional effect. Ask your spouse to realize the importance of the problem and remind him or her that the best way of pleasing you is to address the issue directly. The positive aspect to being a pleaser-soother is that this person seeks to build the unity of the group by coming through for others. But if the pleaser-soother gets locked into this role he or she may easily become an avoider, especially if family tension and conflict are high.

2. Truth-Teller

The truth-teller is a person who is usually going to tell it "like it is," even if it might sound hurtful. This person does not hold back in terms of opinions and feelings. This person's main objective is to face whatever difficulty is confronting the marriage and to deal with it directly. The truth-teller believes that conflict is not bad, even though it may be unpleasant. The worst thing that can happen for this person is to avoid the problem and not deal with it. A truth-teller who is married to a pleaser-soother will often feel frustrated by his or her spouse's approach to conflict, and can easily label it as avoiding. The pleaser-smoother can easily see his or her spouse as too critical and judgmental. If you're married to a truth-teller the best approach is the direct one: explain your own style concerning conflict. You may also need to commit to directly saying what you want out of a specific situation.

The truth-teller brings much to any relationship because honesty can cut through to what is really going on and it can bring people to deal with hidden or unconscious issues. The negative side to being a truth-teller shows itself in the frustration that occurs when one's position or feelings are being ignored. At this point the truth-teller can become strident, feeling like the "bad guy" all the time.

3. Delayer-Avoider

The delayer-avoider is a person who clearly does not want to deal with conflict head-on. This person has learned that if you wait long enough, many problems either go away or solve themselves. This person also believes that conflict has many toxic side effects, like yelling, name calling, sarcasm, belittling, and hitting below the belt. The delayer-avoider has seen mostly the negatives of conflict in his or her own family of origin. As such, this person will spend a good deal of time waiting out conflictual times. This often angers the other spouse, especially if there is a feeling that the conflicts never get dealt with. If you're married to a delayer-avoider it's best to realize that somewhere along the line this person was harmed by the way conflict was handled in his or her family of origin, to the point of just not wanting to deal with problems. If you are a delayer-avoider you might be afraid of arguing with your spouse for fear of using the toxic communications that you learned as a child. The best thing here is to talk to your spouse about what is going on with you internally when there is an argument. If you have experienced significant emotional damage, it might be helpful for you to explore some counseling with your spouse so that you can together change the pattern.

4. Lawyer-Debater

The lawyer-debater's first approach to conflict is to take the defense position. He or she may even interrupt the other spouse's early description of the problem and begin to embark on a vigorous defense. And when the lawyer-debater has a problem it is common to ask questions as if a trial is underway. "Why did you do this at such and such a time," or "Why do you say that about me. It isn't true and I'll show you why." The lawyer-debater believes that conflict means you can't let people push you around. If you do, they will trample all over you. In this view the best defense is a good offense. This person doesn't avoid a fight, but will come out swinging when conflict begins. If you're a lawyer-debater realize that this is a style that you learned in order to defend yourself against what you thought were either superior or potentially overwhelming forces. Realize that your spouse is not one of these forces and that you don't have to protect yourself this way. If you're married to a lawyer-debater try to signal your spouse that you're not trying to prove him or her wrong, that all you want to do is to talk about a problem. Talk first about how you contribute to the problem and then ask your partner to address the problem from his or her perspective.

WHEN CONFLICT ESCALATES

Remember the model of successful conflict resolution in the previous chapter? There comes a point where we face the choice between building a bridge back to our spouse or continuing a process of harmful communication. When conflict starts a couple first attempts to solve it. Once an argument starts there are two choices: resolution or escalation. Escalation occurs when one spouse feels either that they're not being listened to, that their significant other is avoiding the problem all together, or that they're being attacked by their partner. Many arguments escalate not because people want to avoid, ignore, or attack each other; they escalate because we often mis-read each other. Also, each of the above styles has a built in "escalator," meaning that each style is capable of being interpreted negatively by the other.

Once a conflict escalates we can revert to more negative and damaging roles or we can make a choice to adopt a more positive and community building role. The following roles address both the negative and positive styles that a couple can choose to adopt when conflict escalates. I use the word "choose" quite consciously since most couples, when they escalate, fall into negative roles quite unconsciously. If you make it a point to consciously choose the role you will play when conflict escalates, you will be much more successful at resolving it.

1. The Complainer-Critic

In this role you feel that all you are doing is complaining about what is wrong. You use phrases like "you always . . ." and "you never . . ." to describe the other's behavior: "You always forget to take the trash out." At the same time your level of frustration is high because you believe that most of the time you are not being listened to.

2. The Cynic

In this role you constantly make sarcastic comments about almost anything your spouse says as the conflict escalates. You may even belittle your spouse's attempts to send a peace signal to you.

3. The Punishing Parent

In this role you first scold your spouse and then when he or she doesn't respond positively, you cut off of your spouse emotionally. You refuse to talk and refuse to consider a request to reconcile. This might go on for days.

4. The Pouting Child

It's hard to have a punishing parent without a pouting child. In this role you sulk for hours or even days, especially when your spouse clearly admits to being wrong after the argument is finished. And at the first sign of renewed conflict you retreat back into this role.

5. The Rage Warrior-Exploder

In this role you let your "anger be your guide" once conflict escalates. You explode, rant, and rave. People in your family may even be a bit afraid of your temper. And you might even feel that the explosive anger was justified by the perceived injustice done to you.

6. The Interrupter

This is the person who will interrupt his or her spouse when conflict escalates, breaking in after only a few words are spoken. Interrupting someone when conflict is escalating is a good way to ensure that conflict continues to escalate.

7. The Pursuer

When conflict escalates this person hates to be ignored and will pursue the other person into different rooms in order to make a point.

8. The Escaper

The escaper basically shuts down emotionally and withdraws physically when conflict escalates. He or she may stay in this mode for days and is usually sensitive to threat or afraid of anger.

ALTERNATIVE POSITIVE ROLES

Your arguments do not have to go the direction of harmful communication and negative roles. If you discover that either of you adopts any of the above negative roles during conflict, the best thing is to talk about it when things calm down. Say what you want from each other when the conflict escalates. Commit to take a time out when you perceive you are becoming locked into a negative role. Then, consciously try to adopt one of the positive roles below. Remember, you have a choice about how you will act. Resolution may seem like the obvious choice, but it takes a lot of work. Negative roles are probably more instinctive to us when conflict begins to escalate. The following roles, when chosen, will allow each of you to feel more loved and respected.

1. Problem-Definer

In this role you define the problem as specifically as you can. You speak for yourself concerning how the problem affects you, using "I" language as much as possible. You connect events with feelings and with the impact they had on you. You also say what you want to see happen and you indicate that you're open to negotiation. "When such and such occurred I felt this way, and as a result this happened. I want the problem to be solved in this way. . . . What do you think?"

2. Bridge-Builder

Adopting this role means that you might say things like this to your spouse when conflict escalates: "I really want to be your friend and resolve this. How can we do this?" It might also mean that you take the other's side for a while in order to signal your positive attempt. "Let me get into your skin so I can understand the problem from your perspective."

3. Feeling-Affirmer

In this role you concentrate on attending to your spouse's feelings so that you do not minimize the impact of the problem. This role requires you to respond first of the other's feelings before you make your own feeling response. This requires a good deal of discipline and self-presence in order to attend to another's feelings, especially when your own feelings might be all in a jumble.

4. Content Validator-Listener

It helps when someone just hears us out and truly listens to what the other is saying without interruption. Truly indicating that you have heard the other person de-escalates the situation and helps the other find an anchor in safety and calm. Saying, "Tell me what is making you so angry," and then really listening can go a long way to resolving conflict.

5. Option Generator

This person realizes that the more options available when facing a problem, the better both spouses will feel. He or she attempts to see as many options as possible once the problem is adequately defined.

CONFLICT RULES

Treat the other with respect by the use of eye contact, calm voice tone, non threatening body posture, and by respectful speech

Listen to the other until you experience the other side. Good listening involves being able to re-state the other's *content, meaning and feelings* in such a way that he/she signals "you got it".

Communicate respect for the person. Make sure that the focus is on a specific behavior, feeling or value. It is important to signal the other that the issue is not about his/her person, but about a specific behavior or statement.

Solve one thing at a time. Don't bring up issues from the past.

Avoid saying things like "you always" and "you never". They only cause the other to escalate.

Be as specific as possible in what you mean and want.

Don't mind read

Don't interrupt

Calm your inner talk

Avoid the four most damaging communication patterns of criticism, defensiveness, contempt and stonewalling.

When you speak try to say the word "you" only once. This is very hard to do since we usually want to accuse or blame the other person.

1. Begin with **content summary**: "Tell me what happened..." or "Tell me what is making you so angry...";

2. Move to **content validation**: "You're saying that..." Keep this going until the other indicates that you have heard correctly his/ her content.

3. Engage **in "emotion coaching"** : John Gottman in his book **Raising an Emotionally Intelligent Child** (Shuster and Shuster, 1995) calls us to be aware of the other's emotions and to recognize feelings as an opportunity for intimacy. Respond with soothing words and behaviors. This communicates safety and respect to the other. "You seem angry."

4. Don't forget **meaning validation**: "I can see that being included means a lot to you..."

Only after you have gone through content, feeling and meaning validation do you move on to state your position and feelings on the matter.

Sometimes it is important to agree to disagree. This can only happen if both parties agree to treat the other with respect.

Once a person is feeling listened to and the tension de-escalated move on to problem solving. If possible, ask the other if he/she has thought of any solutions. Offer yours as well.

A FINAL WORD ABOUT ANGER

Anger is one of those feelings that has an especially strong impact on people. Perhaps in our own family history anger was used to protect us from danger. A father or mother might have spoken harshly to children in an attempt to protect them from danger. Whatever the case, anger seems to get our attention like no other feeling can. It's not neutral and neither is our response to anger. There are three ways to express anger: direct and congruent, indirect and passive, and aggressive.

Aggressive anger is never helpful in a marriage relationship where two spouses expect to be equals to one another and to have a relationship based on trust and safety. Aggressive anger harms the equality of the relationship and destroys the safety of the marital bond. There is always an implicit threat to use this type of anger against another person. This is why it's controlling, because people will modify their behavior because they are afraid of the other's anger.

Aggressive anger can be divided into physically aggressive and emotionally aggressive anger. Physically aggressive anger shows itself in physical threats, physical intimidation with one's body, throwing of objects, punching walls, pushing, shoving, and hitting.

Emotionally aggressive anger shows itself in direct insults, name calling, put downs, criticism, sarcasm, interrogating, shouting, and yelling. There is an obvious link between physically aggressive anger and emotionally aggressive anger in that emotional aggression is almost always present in domestic violence. But there are a high percentage of people who engage in emotionally aggressive anger who don't become physically violent. This type of anger is really about power and control, where one person uses anger to maintain dominance over the other.

Indirect and passive anger is often expressed through teasing, sarcasm, dirty looks, scowls, cynical comments, and the like. This type of anger is more common between married people; we act out our anger rather than talk about it. If asked to do something, we'll do it, but slowly so as to anger our spouse. If we get chewed out by a superior at work we might chew out our spouse or a child instead of directly talking about how we feel about getting a reprimand.

While it might be more common, this type of anger, over time, can also harm the relationship, slowly eroding the foundation of trust, safety, and mutual respect. A couple who wants to maximize their own marital potential would do well to consider whether this type of anger is present in their relationship. While this type of anger is also about gaining power and control, both spouses often feel that they cannot win the struggle. Still they continue to take shots at each other. It's a skirmish that cannot be won. A couple can be cynical and sarcastic with each other, and even take pot shots at each other; yet they do not fear that the anger will escalate to the point where one spouse is fearful of the other.

Direct and Congruent Anger seeks to connect events with feelings and describes the impact on the person without blaming, criticizing, becoming cynical, shouting, etc. This type of anger allows anger to be a feeling rather than a justification for retaliation. It's congruent because a person seeks to clearly express what he or she is feeling on the inside and connect it with what is happening in the external world. Also, this form of anger is directed toward very specific events and doesn't implicate the entire person. There is a big difference between hearing, "You're so stupid for doing such and such," and "When you did such and such I became angry because it caused me to be late for work." A couple that consistently strives for the direct and congruent expression of anger will maximize the potential for a successful marriage.

Do You Have a Problem With Anger?

You may have a problem with anger if the following are true about you:

- You have sometimes or often thrown things when you become angry
- You have grabbed or hit your spouse or used intimidating body postures when angry
- People have told you that they are afraid of your anger
- Your first reaction to conflict is to become irritated, defensive and/or angry
- You find that you cannot control when you are going to blow up.
- You usually tease or use cynical comments toward those you love.
- Your spouse has told you that the relationship may be in trouble if the pattern of your anger persists.
- You have tried to control your anger but find that it is very difficult to do so.

Take Responsibility for Your Anger. Sometimes the way you get angry is a problem in itself and requires special attention. A major criteria for seeking the help of a individual or marriage counselor should be:

- if you and your spouse have been stuck in the same pattern of escalating conflict and anger for some time;
- if the way you get angry keeps your spouse or your children from approaching you the majority of the time; all they do is to try to appease you and turn down your "anger thermostat";
- if people in your household are afraid that you cannot control your anger and you have become physically angry in the past.

If any of these are present in your relationship consider getting help by utilizing the services of a trained and qualified counselor.

A Slice of Life

In the beginning, before children, Laura found it easy to talk to her husband Frank about problems in their relationship. He was usually easygoing and able to understand her feelings on most matters. He was also quick to make suggestions and take responsibility by really listening to her suggestions.

Now, with three children ages ten, seven, and five Laura found married life to be much more complicated. They were both extremely busy and their children demanded much of their attention. They had little time for each other, and in the time they had Laura found herself bringing to Frank more and more problems. She became aware of this when Frank snapped at her one day, "Now what's the problem!"

Their arguing had increased as well. Both had a negative side to the way they engaged each other. After the argument started Laura would scold and tell Frank what his problem was. Frank would become cynical and eventually blow up at his wife, telling her that he couldn't take this anymore. Laura would then withdraw and not talk to Frank for two to three days.

On the days when there was less stress they were able to get along with each other and even enjoy the other's company. It was during these times that they talked about the patterns they had gotten into and how they wanted to change the negative way they related when tension increased. Frank could identify that he didn't like being scolded and Laura was able to tell him she didn't like his criticism and anger when they fought. Both indicated a desire to change but were not quite sure what to do differently. Both feared a repeat of the same old patterns. They both agreed to try to refrain from escalating the argument. One new thing they came up with was that each of them could call a time out during an argument as long as that person agreed to come back and finish the discussion. Both were hopeful that they could change their negative pattern but both were also a bit afraid that they were stuck in a negative conflict cycle.

AWARENESS IN ACTION

When we feel pushed into a corner, or when we're under a lot of stress, it seems that there is a tendency to fight dirty or to "rant and rave." Sometimes we just get into an irritable zone where the slightest comment from our spouse elicits a negative reaction.

- Does the above slice of life appear at all familiar to you? What is your own pattern of conflict resolution?
- What positive things do you do to resolve conflict? What negative patterns do each of you bring to an argument?
- Do you see any of the above negative roles in either of your conflict resolution styles? Do you see any of the positives?
- If you decided to act differently concerning the way you handled conflict how would you be different? For instance would you take a time out, or talk about your feelings? Try to describe in specific terms what you want to work on.

THE SPIRITUAL DIMENSION: CREATIVE TENSION

It was Martin Luther King, Jr., who used the phrase "creative tension" to describe the goals of his nonviolent approach to racial tension. His approach was rooted in respect for all people regardless of their sex or race and in taking a clear, firm nonviolent stand against injustice. His idea of "creative tension" and nonviolence was founded on a deep spirituality. He believed that through this process those who were in power would have to acknowledge those who were the victims of injustice. His approach is credited with changing the views of American society in the 1960s regarding race relations.

It's possible for a marriage to embody the spiritual principles of "creative tension" when a couple has conflicts. A creative resolution of marital problems is also founded on the absolute respect for the other person and a commitment to resolve arguments nonviolently.This means avoiding the language of put downs, sarcasm, criticism and the many other ways we hit below the belt. It sometimes means living with a problem where there is no immediate solution. Most importantly, it means a true sharing of power between the two spouses, where there is an acknowledgment that neither one wishes to overpower or control the other. This, of course, takes a lot of "blood, sweat and tears"—as well as prayer—to make happen. But it is worth the effort.

Answer Honestly then Share....

The skills I want to most develop are....

One thing I like about myself emotionally is...

The thing I most fear about conflict is....

10

RECOGNIZING PATTERNS OF BEHAVIOR AND FACING YOUR FEARS

In marriage, one can't do anything alone, not even suffer.

–MARY ADAMS

The story is told in the Gospel of Luke about a possessed man who left his family to reside in the local cemetery (Lk 8:26-39). As Luke tells it, the man is so tormented by demons that the townsfolk resort to chaining him to the tombstones. But under the torment the man would break free of his bonds.

Then Jesus the master healer expels the demons and restores the man to complete health. Once cured, the man wants to follow Jesus and become a disciple. Jesus allows him to become a disciple but sends the man back to his family to share with his friends and family the story of his possession and healing by Jesus.

Demons can come in all shapes and sizes. As children we are taught to believe that demons actually exist in physical form, but as adults we know that the most dangerous demons are the ones we imagine. In this figurative use of the word demon we are talking about the times in our lives when we become obsessed with an idea or become compulsive about a habit that begins to eventually control us and damage our relationships. These "demons" often take the form of things we fear the most. And sometimes the things we fear the most influence the quality of our lives and our relationships.

Sometimes like the man in the story, we are tormented by forces that we believe to be beyond our control. Sometimes the way we behave under the influence of these forces causes us to isolate ourselves from our family and friends. It is telling that at the end of the story, Jesus sends the man back to his own family, even though he asks to become a disciple. Jesus' healing of this man in some sense involves reconciliation with the man's family of origin. All of us have unresolved issues with our families of origin that ask to be resolved one way or the other, and they often manifest themselves in the form of fears and anxieties.

PATTERNS OF BEHAVIOR

Have you ever wondered how you developed into who you are, a complex mix of emotions and personality traits? Psychologists tell us that many of these traits develop at a very early age when we are bonding with our parents or other significant adults. At this early stage of our lives we have a deep need for reassurance, nurturing, safety, and emotional contact. If a parent is physically absent or emotionally distant, the child will find a number of ways to respond to the anxiety this creates. These responses eventually become patterns of behavior, or in the language of one school of psychology, "patterns of attachment." These patterns apply not only to our relationships with our parents, but to other relationships as well.

Most of us come into our adult years with a combination of healthy and unhealthy attachment patterns. When we marry, we tend to carry these patterns over to our relationships with our spouses. They are usually driven by either a need for our spouse to be closer to us or by a sense of being smothered.

Let's examine some of the more common patterns that shape our way of relating to our spouse, some of which can develop without our full awareness:

1. Angry Withdrawal

People who get caught up in this pattern often feel hurt and anger without understanding why. It may be because they feel their spouse isn't present enough. Or it may be because they are looking for approval from their spouse whom they think is withholding approval and/ or affection. This sense on one spouse's part can sometimes initiate a cycle in which the other spouse also responds with anger and withdrawal.

2. Compulsive Caregiving

In this pattern one spouse consistently places the needs of the other spouse before his or her own. This pattern emerges from the belief that being a caretaker will motivate the other person to provide the level of emotional contact desired. Someone caught up in this pattern will exhibit a great deal of sensitivity to the partner and a good deal of anxiety that the other person will not be happy. One's sense of self-worth is derived from doing things for and making sure that other is happy. In marriage, this pattern translates into not being able to say no to one's spouse for fear of losing approval and validation. It can lead to an even higher level of personal anxiety when one's partner is unhappy, stressed out, or angry.

3. Compulsive Self-Reliance

This pattern is the opposite of compulsive caregiving. Here there is a sense that one's needs are met best if one spouse doesn't depend on the other. There might have been an early disappointment in life where the person felt the acute absence of a caregiver and decided to face things alone. Or perhaps the family life was so chaotic that the child simply had to fend for him or herself. Whatever the case, this pattern suggests that too much closeness can be dangerous and that one needs to hide one's anxieties and protect them from discovery. Thus, to the observer, this person will appear quite self-reliant, perhaps even charming, but always in control. It is difficult for this person to form close relationships and show one's deeper insecurities to a spouse. It's not uncommon for a person who has the compulsive caregiving pattern to marry someone who has the compulsive self-reliance pattern, for the profile of self-reliance drives the fears of the caregiver that affection will one day be completely withdrawn.

4. Compulsive Care-Seeking

This pattern is characterized by a dependence on one's spouse and wanting to be taken care of like a child again. There is a sense of being helpless and a greater fear and anxiety of being cut off. When this person's stress increases due to troubles at work or on the home front there is a great deal of anxiety and many requests for comfort. This "high maintenance" care can be a pattern that only emerges fully once a marriage is underway. What the compulsive care-seeking person fears most is desertion by the caregiver. There is a great fear of being left or of not being good enough. This pattern also is characterized by a chronic low self-esteem on the part of the one seeking care.

5. Appropriate Attachments

The healthy and appropriate way out of these patterns is to articulate one's needs, anxieties, and fears and to communicate them so that one's anxieties about the future and how these needs will be met can be calmed. This pattern is characterized by the maintenance of emotional balance even when one spouse is angry with the other. There is a sense of being interdependent, meaning that a person can both meet one's own needs independent of the spouse, but also show one's vulnerability by allowing another to be caring. In a marriage this pattern also has a fair amount of give and take and negotiating between the two spouses on how the needs of each will get met.

FACING OUR FEARS

Have you ever noticed that when you are afraid you have a harder time concentrating, staying on task, performing up to your potential, not to mention relaxing? Arthur Deming, the great management guru, had as one of his first principles for maximizing human potential: "drive out all fear." This is a principle that is often easier said than done.

The thing about fear is this: we have two choices when confronted by our deepest fears. We can either face them or run from them. When we face them we usually win a greater sense of self and solid identity. This is hard work. When we run from them we usually employ the psychological mechanisms of denial, rationalization and defensiveness in order to justify our decision to avoid facing our fears.

The following represent some of the deeper fears that we will face in life. Each fear is rooted in some way in one of the attachment patterns described above. With each fear you will identify an accompanying negative belief that often reinforces and sustains the cycle of fear. Finally, some suggestions will be given concerning how to face the particular fear and what you can do about it. Most of us we will identify with one or two of the deeper fears; some of us might identify with all of them.

Fear of Rejection/Abandonment

Abandonment is the other side of belonging. The belief associated with this fear says that the people the closest to you will either leave you or find you wanting. When you have this fear you don't trust that you belong to whatever group you're in. You're always looking for the first sign of trouble, the first sign that someone will show you the door. You might even misinterpret someone's body posture, a frown, what you think is a scowl or dirty look. When this happens you might say to yourself, "What did I do wrong?"

This fear can lead a person to work very hard at gaining the acceptance of others, even to the point of sacrificing personal needs. There is an inordinate "need to be liked," because when we are liked we are then accepted. Abandonment fears are common in people who have come from homes where one or both parents used emotional cut-off to control behavior. "If you don't do what I want, I won't be accessible to you" is the message behind this fear. There are some who act out of this fear in an openly anxious manner and are quite sensitive to any threat of being cut off or excluded. The person who is sensitive to being excluded might join many groups and have a difficult time saying no, for fear that their "no" will lead to rejection. This fear also leads to a deep insecurity and can cause intense jealousy.

Fear of Failure and Incompetence

Have you ever bemoaned the fact that you were just not smart enough, creative enough, or good enough to get ahead at work? Or have you felt that you don't deserve the success you already have, that one day people will discover you are a fraud impersonating a successful person? If so, then you have just named one of your fears, the fear of failure and incompetence. This fear is born out of the belief that we can gain love and acceptance through performing well. This is a very common fear in our society today, which places a high emphasis on competence and performance in work, leisure, and home life.

People who have this fear can come from very "normal" families, but there is usually the presence of perfectionism on the part of one or both of the parents. Perfectionism creates an environment where there are very high moral and educational standards. Children who are raised with a perfectionistic standard can easily develop a feeling of inadequacy, especially if they find themselves failing to meet their own expectations as well as the expectations of their parents.

There is also a good deal of anger generated by this fear, anger at oneself for not being good enough, and "sideways" anger that seeps out of the cracks and gets directed at our loved ones. Procrastination is also a big problem for people beset by this fear; because they believe that they can never do a job good enough, they put off the completion of the project. The person facing this fear somehow has learned to associate affirmation and love with performance: the better you do in sports and in school the more positive feedback you will get from us as your parents. In this family failure is simply unacceptable.

This is a fear that affects people who are establishing their careers or who have had some real experience of workplace setback or failure. Someone who has a fear of failing will have a difficult time relaxing and having fun. Being hard on oneself comes with this territory, and you might find yourself complaining more than you want; you may even then become defensive when your spouse gives you suggestions about doing better. Your spouse might even grow tired of listening to the ever present anxiety concerning failure. The other major problem that can arise out of this fear is a difficulty with the setting of limits concerning how much and long you work. Gaining affirmation through work and performance is a recipe for creating a workaholic.

Fears of Not Enough Intimacy, Too Much Intimacy

These fears can be set side by side since they arise out of the same theme of intimacy. With these fears we feel either cut off from love or overwhelmed by love. The person who feels cut off from love has an abiding sense of never being able to receive enough affirmation and acceptance and fears that he or she will live a life of loneliness. This person may become either a caretaker or a care seeker. He or she may experience a spouse as inaccessible or distant and make various attempts to communicate and become closer, only to be rebuffed and hurt. This person also may feel that the quality of friendship is lacking and may have anxiety concerning being able to form close and lasting bonds with others.

On the other side of the spectrum is the person who feels overwhelmed and smothered by attempts of others to become emotionally close. This person may have the compulsive self-reliant pattern and is used to being independent and doesn't look to others to meet many of his or her needs. This person may have a high need for a lot of alone time, and may express dissatisfaction with close associates who show their deeper emotional selves. This person may have come from a family where close emotional support was either lacking or inconsistent, and therefore learned to insulate him or herself from the lack of intimacy.

Fears of not enough intimacy or being smothered by intimacy can cause a couple to do a "dance of intimacy" where the spouse who is more "intimacy seeking" pursues the spouse who is more "intimacy fearing." When this occurs there is usually a lot of marital dissatisfaction.

Fear of Conflict

This might be the marital "mother of all fears" because a fear of conflict can prevent a couple from solving even the most basic problems that arise. Often, the person who is a caretaker or peacemaker will show a fear of conflict and sometimes an outright avoidance of it. This fear usually has its roots in a person's primary family of origin where one learned that conflict is a toxic thing to be avoided at all costs. People who are peacemakers often fear conflict. Their experience has been one of unsolved, frequent conflict, verbally and perhaps also physically abusive. A person who fears conflict in a marriage can avoid his or her spouse, especially when emotions run high over a problem.

Six Steps to Facing Fear

Unfaced fears can lead to all sorts of harmful things: addiction, inappropriate anger, an abiding feeling of insecurity, a "driven" personality, eating problems, and poor conflict resolution skills. The following might help you in identifying your fears with your spouse:

1. Name your fears

Giving voice to the unconscious fears you may have is the first place to start. Naming what is going on with you allows you to create options and exercise greater control over your life.

2. Realize that your worst fears often don't come true

When they do you have more skills than you realize to deal with them. Unfaced fears are like shadows we cast that appear larger than life. When we turn and face them and shine the light of reflection on them they almost always shrink to a size that is manageable.

3. See your spouse as your ally in facing your fears

Think about what you need from your spouse in order to talk about your fears. A listening ear? Advice? A sounding board? It's important to define your spouse's role if you're going to take on this task. Sometimes you will be confused by what you want from your spouse in this regard; hang in there and trust that your instincts will tell you what you want.

4. Deal with your anger

Don't use anger to control or to defend yourself. If you have identified yourself as having any of the attachment patterns listed above it's possible that you use your anger either to protect yourself or to express your anxiety when your stress is too high. This type of anger can be destructive, not only to you but to your relationship. This is anger as a defense, not as a feeling. It keeps people away from you. Commit to doing better with your anger, and if you need to talk to someone about it, take the risk to do better.

5. If your fear involves your spouse, commit to talking this out

Be reciprocal with each other. Can you reassure your spouse about some fear? Are you willing to face how you participate in the maintaining of the fear if it's an issue?

6. Consider getting into marriage counseling

Seek counseling with your spouse if the fear and problem become ever present and unmanageable. Early detection of marital problems is actually a sign of health. The quicker you act to solve the problem effectively the better your marriage will be.

A SLICE OF LIFE

Chad and Jennifer have been married for fifteen years. Their oldest daughter is now a freshman in high school. Just five years ago Jennifer was diagnosed with breast cancer and had a radical mastectomy, followed by radiation treatments for six weeks. After the treatments were finished she had reconstructive surgery. She has been cancer free for five years and the doctors assure her that her prognosis continues to look very good.

Since their oldest daughter became a teen Chad has noticed a gradual but clear change in Jennifer. Over the last year and a half Jennifer has gained about 20 lbs and has become more snappy to those in her family. Her relationship with her daughter has gone from good to strained. They seem to fight all the time.

What is more, Chad has also noticed that Jennifer's consumption of alcohol has gone up considerably over the last year. She used to have an occasional drink. Now she is drinking up to four glasses of wine an evening. Chad has quietly taken to marking the wine bottle in the refrigerator so as to monitor her consumption level.

When he has raised his concerns with Jennifer she has been stubborn and defensive. Jennifer describes as "ridiculous" his concerns about her drinking and becomes quite defensive when he tries to talk to her about her weight. She accuses him of being insensitive and heartless when he attempts to share his concerns. She has said to him on a number of occasions, "Take me as I am. Either love me or leave me." Those discussions usually end up in tears and Chad feeling like he is the bad guy.

Chad thinks that Jennifer has become more depressed in the last year and a half and may even be jealous of their oldest daughter moving into puberty. When he said this to Jennifer she accused him of playing "psychologist" and told him that until he had a life threatening illness he would never understand how she felt.

Their teen daughter has begun to catch on to the growing tension between the two, and even to Jennifer's increased drinking. Chad is beginning to withdraw more from Jennifer. He realizes that this can only make things worse, but he is feeling helpless about what to do. He even called Jennifer's doctor, who agreed that Jennifer might be depressed. The doctor recommended that Chad talk to Jennifer again and persuade her to address her depression. "Easier said than done" Chad said to himself after talking to the doctor.

AWARENESS IN ACTION

Sometimes we become our worst enemies because of our inability to deal with our fears and anxieties. Marriage is about sharing our vulnerabilities and underdeveloped selves with our spouses. Yet sometimes we fail to do so because of embarrassment, shame, or fear of criticism. Could you, or have the two of you ever had a dialog similar to the one described above? In the case above it's possible that

Jennifer has some unexamined fears associated with her cancer recovery.

- Sometimes life's troubles can rattle our sense of safety and security. Is it easy or difficult to share your vulnerabilities with your spouse?
- Do you recognize yourself in any of the attachment patterns listed above?
- Why, if we are life partners, do we sometimes not communicate our fears and worries to our spouse?
- Are there any fears in this chapter with which you identify? Are there others not listed here that occupy your time and attention? Can you share them with your spouse?

THE SPIRITUAL DIMENSION: LETTING GO OF FEAR TO TRUST

In the Gospel of Luke the opposite of faith is not disbelief but fear. The Jesus that Luke presents seems to understand the human psyche very well. Again and again Jesus suggests to his followers that fear holds us back and that it robs us of our full potential. In the story of the calming of the sea (Lk 8:22-25) we find the disciples crossing the lake in the boat while Jesus sleeps. A storm comes upon them threatening to swamp the boat, and of course the disciples become afraid. They wake Jesus who challenges them about their faith. He then calms the storm.

Another way to look at this story is this: perhaps Jesus challenged his disciples not only to trust God, but to trust as well their own instincts and skills. After all, they had been on the lake many times before and were most likely skilled and experienced sailors.

What about you? Do you believe that God is present to your own inner instincts and skills? Do you trust that or are you afraid of believing in yourself? One of the most important shifts in adult life comes when we understand that God is "within" our experiences and instincts as much as God is external to ourselves. How would it change you if you began to trust your instincts and feelings as indications of the presence of God?

Answer Honestly then Share....

When I'm feeling down I need...

When I'm afraid I sometimes want to run or fight by....

I feel safest when....

11

KNOWING HOW TO
SOLVE PROBLEMS

To keep your marriage
brimming, with love in the
loving cup, whenever you're
wrong, admit it; whenever
you're right, shut up.
–OGDEN NASH

One bumper sticker says: "Jesus is the answer."
Another reads: "What's the question?" A third:
"What's the problem?" Still another: "If you're
not part of the solution you're part of the
problem." A visitor from another planet, upon
reading these four sayings might conclude that
we Americans are fixated on problem solving.
Yet with all this focus why do we have so many
problems? Go figure.

Married couples know instinctively that
effective conflict resolution skills are an
important part of a successful marriage.
Surveys continually cite poor conflict resolution
as a major cause of marital breakdown. So it
makes sense that the better able the two of
you are to solve problems in a timely fashion

the happier your marriage will be. Easier said than done, but perhaps easier to accomplish than you realize.

Successful vs. Unsuccessful Conflict Resolution

Just about all of us have been in arguments that didn't go anywhere or do anything for us except make us tired and discouraged. Many couples ask themselves: "Why do we keep arguing about the same things?" Part of the answer lies in understanding the difference between successful and unsuccessful conflict resolution. The following shows these differences.

Successful Conflict Resolution

1. Problem or complaint is raised by one spouse to the other.
2. Initial attempt at solution. If none then . . .
3. Escalation into arguing.
4. Bridge building attempts by both spouses that involve:
   a. attempt to understand other's position and feelings,
   b. attempt to signal other of hope for a positive outcome,
   c. attempt to signal other of desire to maintain friendship,

  d. refusal to hit below the belt by criticizing, ridiculing, or belittling the other.
5. Problem clarification and option generation.

Unsuccessful Conflict Resolution

1. Problem or complaint is raised by one spouse to the other.
2. Initial attempt at solution. If none then . . .
3. Escalation into arguing.
4. Emotional distancing and alienation through persistent defensiveness, criticism, belittling of the other's position, and disregard for the other.
5. Further escalation of anger and hurt characterized by shouting, name calling, sometimes shoving and hitting.
6. Argument ends either by one person giving in or by two people avoiding each other. Issue is not settled, to be revisited at a later date.

Looking at the above descriptions we can see that both successful and unsuccessful conflicts start the same way but begin to deviate as the argument escalates. Successful couples engage in more bridge building behaviors and statements and are able to de-escalate the argument to the point of solving the problem. All of us want to solve problems effectively when they occur in our marriage. No one looks forward to the jagged hurt feelings that occur when we have an argument that goes nowhere. In order to maximize our ability to manage our conflicts well we need to understand a little bit about how our own personality influences the way we solve problems.

WHAT STOPS BRIDGE BUILDING?

Problems often become greater than they seem and escalate into arguments between a couple. We also know that successful spouses somehow stop the escalation and build bridges back to one another. There are three things that prevent a person from engaging in successful bridge building. They have to do with the personal issues you bring into an attempt to solve a problem.

1. Your own meta-issues and filters from your childhood:

The previous chapter on communication referred to the deeper issues and messages about ourselves that we carry around and that influence how we perceive another's communication. These meta-issues serve as filters for us and influence the way we hear another's communication. If we are sensitive about being excluded then we will listen for a threat to exclude us. If you were dominated or controlled when you were a child, either through physical or verbal abuse, then you will listen for a threat to dominate in the present moment. If you felt inadequate as a child then you will listen for any possible messages that you are inadequate now. Or you might unconsciously just want someone to take care of you and embed that message in your daily communications. Unvoiced and unmet needs can become meta-issues in your life because of your perceived inability to get them met. And most important, if your experience of anger in your family of origin was that it was toxic and threatening, you may in your present moment listen for any hint of anger in the other's voice. And you might seek to avoid the anger and just not deal with the problem.

Another difficulty with the meta-issues is that they often get communicated through the use of voice tonality and body postures, the nonverbals of communication. Thus, your spouse can ask you to shut the window, but in a way where the tone of voice communicates a demand that you perceive as dominant because your filters have you listening for dominance. And because you no longer want to be dominated like you were in childhood, you respond not to the actual request but to the perceived communication given through the voice tonality. When you respond accordingly, an argument ensues. And the two of you begin to fight on the level of your meta-issues, which represent your worst fears. All of this, of course, lies on a level just below your awareness so it is difficult to understand and stop once the argument begins.

2. The tendency to defend:

It might be part of our genetic makeup but our human psyche has equipped us with many ways to defend ourselves. This is because our egos seek to be protected from any sort of threat, real or perceived. When our spouse brings us a problem we may often respond instinctively with irritation or anger. We may begin to rationalize or blame. Or, we may just avoid the issue and not deal with it. These are usually first, instinctive responses to problems. They represent, in the best light, our need for safety and rest. We just don't want to be bothered by a problem. But your spouse might not know that and very innocently bring a problem to you. You then respond in a defensive manner, with irritation and your voice tonality communicates that irritation to your spouse. Your spouse, because of his or her own meta-issues, perceives an unresolved theme and responds accordingly. An argument escalates, not over the initial problem but over the way you responded or became defensive. And if you're not careful feelings are hurt because each of you continues to defend yourselves by blaming, being angry, and the like.

3. Stress:

It's a well-known adage in the therapy culture that when a person is under stress there is a tendency to revert to a more dysfunctional way of communicating. Not too many people, when stressed out, will communicate in a more loving and caring manner. Usually, when you're stressed, you will be more snappy, more irritable, and you will have a tendency to go back to what you learned in your own family of origin about conflict resolution. And if you learned to blame, to use anger to defend yourself when confronted, to put down, or to avoid, chances are you'll want to go back to those same behaviors. This is true even if you have decided to learn a different way to communicate. Part of this is because our brains have formed clear neural pathways for the old behaviors due to the sheer amount of repetitive behavior in childhood. So if you experienced being blamed a thousand times in childhood, the pathway of blame opens up when you're stressed and tired. And if you follow those old pathways you and your spouse can get on the escalator of harmful conflict resolution.

DEFINING THE PROBLEM

Let's assume that it's possible for the two of you to understand how your own meta-issues, tendencies to defend yourselves, and stress influence the way you communicate. Now you can go on to actually defining the problem that you need to discuss. But it's important to know what you want from the other person and when the problem will be solved. Therapists call this a well formed outcome. It's a way of asking about your immediate goals and expectations concerning problem resolution. It makes sense to have a well formed outcome, but there are many couples who simply don't take the time to really think about the problem and describe it.

Often each spouse will have a different take on what the problem is. If you give yourself time to talk about what the problem is, you maximize your chances of resolving it. However, if each of you makes assumptions about the other's point of view your attempt at problem solving can develop into a real conflict. Remember, not all problems we face need to become conflictual. Also, this process encourages the taking of individual responsibility. This process can be best described through a series of questions that you and your spouse can ask when you face conflict.

A WELL-FORMED OUTCOME: A PROCESS OF PROBLEM DEFINITION

1. First, are you aware of your own meta-issues and/or unvoiced needs? Are these in any way influencing the way you

either communicate about a problem or listen to your spouse communicate about a problem? If so, take some time to surface these issues and needs and ask to speak with your spouse about them. Sometimes these issues and needs are so powerful that you might have to ask a third party to serve as a mediator/listener. This person is often a marriage therapist.

2. How do each of you define the problem? Can you describe the problem using only "I" language? Can you both agree on how the problem is defined?

3. How does this problem affect you personally, what are the consequences for you if the problem persists? For instance, are you losing sleep, worrying too much, etc.

4. If the problem involves behavior on the part of your spouse be sure to connect behaviors, feelings, and consequences. Be sure to describe only one specific behavior. Example: "When you tell me you'll be home by six and you come home at eight I feel worried and angry (feeling) because I'm not sure where you are and I can't relax (consequence).

5. How does each of you contribute to the problem? Speak only for yourselves: "my part of this problem is that I. . . ." The best way to successfully conclude an

argument is for each person to talk about how he or she contributes to it and then describe how he or she can solve it.

6. Generate solutions. Again speak for yourself. What can each of you do to solve the problem? The greater the problem the greater the need to generate a solution. Generate as many solutions as possible. Spouses often limit themselves by stopping after only a few. Once you have an acceptable number of solutions begin a process of prioritizing which results in one or two solutions that you could see yourselves implementing.

A SLICE OF LIFE

Peggy and Chris have been married for fifteen years. Each was married once previously. Peggy's first marriage lasted for five years and Chris' first marriage lasted only two years. Both of them married when they were right out of high school. Neither has children from their first marriage and together they have two children ages thirteen and eleven. When they met each other they dated for two years before marrying. They both valued honesty and their friends would describe their marriage as "ideal." But the reality was a bit more sober.

Over the last few years Chris has been working longer hours and he and Peggy have gradually gotten more out of touch with each other. Then, their oldest child, Nathan, began having discipline problems in middle school. They began to argue over the right direction to take with him. Peggy would want to discuss options with Chris, but he would sometimes shut down and not want to deal with the problems. Peggy would then become quite angry with his avoidant behavior.

Peggy's world was shattered just recently when Chris confided in her that he had developed an office romance with a coworker. It had not yet become sexual but Chris conceded that it could if he let it. He had decided to be honest with Peggy since he had become more uncomfortable with the secret. Peggy was devastated since her first marriage had ended because of an affair. She had always told herself that she would not let herself be a victim to another affair. And here was Chris telling her about the office relationship and that he wanted to try to work things out. She was angry and hurt by Chris' action and wasn't sure which way to turn. In many ways she felt abandoned by Chris yet understood that he wanted to address the problem and work on the relationship. Part of her wanted to work on things; another part of her wanted to tear into him for making things so bad.

AWARENESS IN ACTION

"If you're not part of the solution, you're part of the problem." Does this saying hold true for your own marital conflicts? Building bridges toward the other, especially in times of conflict, can be one of the hardest things done by a man or woman. It's natural that we want others to take our side and sympathize with our position. But when the person you look to for support is fighting with you this can become a very difficult task.

- How successful do you think you and your spouse are at building bridges toward one another in times of conflict?
- Does conflict scare you? If so, can you identify what your fears are concerning conflict?
- How can your spouse help make conflict more safe?
- In the above slice of life Peggy and Chris were unable to resolve conflict over how to handle their oldest child, and things seemed to get worse for them. If you were giving them advice what would you tell them to do differently?

THE SPIRITUAL DIMENSION: CONFLICT CAN BE HOLY

Most of us fear conflict and seek to minimize its effects on us. Yet one of the twentieth century's leading figures, Martin Luther King, Jr., used the phrase "creative tension" to describe how people who are engaged in conflict can work toward solutions. His way was the way of nonviolent protest based on respect for the dignity of all people, especially those oppressed by an unjust system and by poverty.

When we are in conflict with someone we begin to feel tension, sometimes great tension. What can make the tension creative is our willingness to honor and respect the other even when we are angry, to not belittle, put down, treat poorly, or trample on his or her rights. "Creative tension" means adopting the view that the God force resides in the deepest parts of the other, and that by dishonoring the other we are dishonoring God and ourselves. "Creative tension" also encourages us to work toward a situation where both parties are winners. It means standing our ground when necessary, but in all things honoring the other as a child of God.

Answer Honestly then Share....

One way you can help me feel safe physically is...

One way you can help me feel safe emotionally is....

When we have a problem I will commit to....

12

KNOWING AND NURTURING YOUR
BOTTOM LINE VALUES

A successful marriage is an
edifice that must be rebuilt
every day.
—ANDRE MAUROIS

Understanding one's bottom line values is one
crucial ingredient for a successful marriage.
Taking responsibility for nurturing these values
is another essential ingredient. Sometimes we
have to speak our own truth concerning these
values. Naming our own truth about these
core values can help a couple to face a subtle
erosion of their marital foundations and get
their marriage back on track. It is far better to
take a proactive stance toward these values
by taking responsibility to see that they are
actively cultivated in your marriage.

This responsibility taking can be described
as creating the core conditions by which a
marriage can grow and thrive. These core
conditions are basically the bottom line values
of respect, trust, honesty, safety, with one very
important skill, that of empathy. Think of the

core conditions as the underlying environment on which the ecosystem of your marriage will grow. If the environment is polluted and fouled then your own marital ecosystem will suffer and perhaps die. And just as we humans face the choice of taking responsibility for ensuring that the earth's air and water are free from pollution, we face the same choice in our marriage. We can create the core conditions that will sustain our marriage or we can pollute our marital environment. The following suggestions offer ways to nurture those bottom line values.

What's Negotiable, What Isn't?

It's important to understand that there are a handful values that form the bedrock of your marriage. If these values are violated the firm ground on which your foundation rests is shaken. Then your marriage is in serious trouble. This doesn't mean there's no hope, but it calls for serious attention. On the plus side, knowing what is not negotiable for you, it's possible that you will feel the freedom to understand that there is a very wide area where many things are negotiable. Here, then are four bottom line non negotiable values that form the bedrock of any mature marriage, as well as suggestions as to how to nurture these bottom line values.

Respect

- Do focus on what your spouse is telling you by maintaining eye contact and giving your full attention.
- Don't interrupt. Let your spouse finish what he or she is saying.
- Don't invade your spouse's emotional space by insisting he or she tell you his or her every thought.
- Don't criticize your spouse in front of others, especially your children.
- Do support your spouse in front of others, especially your children. If you have a disagreement take it behind closed doors to iron out.
- Don't watch TV when having a serious conversation with your spouse. Neither of you can compete with the rapidly changing images of TV, and your eye contact will wander back to the television. This will send a mixed message to your spouse. Instead, decide on when and where the two of you will talk, turn the TV off, and then address the issues at hand.
- Don't ignore your spouse or your children. Being ignored or invisible is one of the hardest things to endure.
- Don't tease in order to communicate your displeasure. Teasing does occur in many relationships but you need to realize that

it can also be a way of expressing anger and frustration. This is especially true for children.

- Do attempt to maintain the five to one rule that states for every one negative interchange between a couple there need to be five positive ones to counter the effects of the negative.

Trust

- Don't sabotage or retaliate when your spouse does something that hurts your feelings or even inconveniences you. While revenge may be fun, it hurts the trust and feels like being hit below the belt.
- Do share information about your day, your feelings, your dreams, your likes and dislikes. Information in a relationship builds trust and rapport between the two of you
- Don't see your spouse as your boss to whom you should report. This will cause resentment and you won't want to share information. Rather, see your spouse as your friend and partner with whom you have an on-going dialog.
- Don't be evasive about your plans, whom you're having lunch with, what you're doing after work hours. If you

travel be forthright and honest about where you're going, your timelines, when you will check in, etc.

- Do commit to talking with your spouse if you experience jealousy concerning relationships that your spouse has with others. Jealousy is sometimes a sign of our own insecurity and a call for us to build our own self-esteem.
- Don't engage in trust breaking behaviors where what you say you'll do doesn't match what you actually do.

Honesty

- Don't placate your spouse by saying you'll do something just to soothe him or her and then not follow through. It's better to be honest about how you feel and what you will do.
- Don't avoid conflict with your spouse. This appears evasive and can be taken as a sign that you don't want to deal with the problem or don't care about it.
- Don't minimize conflict by saying things like, "It's not that bad."
- Do say what is on your mind and how you're feeling about a given situation or problem.

Safety

- Don't respond with anger or irritation when your spouse brings issues for discussion to you.
- Do take responsibility for any anger that can be termed "explosive" where you "blow up" or go "ballistic." This type of anger makes people feel afraid and controlled by you. Your anger is yours, not anyone else's. If you are afraid of your anger then this should be a signal that safety, as a core condition, is being compromised. Sometimes counseling is required to address the underlying issues that lead to this expression of anger.
- Don't respond with sarcasm or cynicism when issues are brought to your attention. This is a subtle form of anger and can begin to undermine the safety, especially with children.
- Don't abuse alcohol and other substances. Alcohol and other substances lower your control center, thus allowing your anger to be expressed in a destructive manner.

Empathy

Empathy means "to have feelings with." To have empathy for another means that you employ your imagination to get into the "skin" of the other person, to feel what the other feels and to understand the world according to the other person's circumstances. Empathy is the life blood of a marriage because it is a learned skill that keeps the love bond strong and supple. To empathize with your spouse is to show that you care very deeply about what is going on in your partner's life. Empathy is a learned skill: it can be taught. We do this when we ask our children to imagine how another feels when that child has done something harmful.

Empathy involves, to some extent, the suspension of your own intellectual and emotional agenda so that you can better understand not only the agenda of the other, but the deeper self of the person.

Why is empathy so powerful? We know that in work groups, support groups and just about any other group there are two things that people report as being essential in making them feel part of the group. They are meaning attribution and caring. Meaning attribution refers to a person's ability to hear the deeper meaning and purpose that motivates another person. It has to do with assisting another to name experiences and dreams of the future. Caring has to do with showing another person that he or she counts and belongs.

It makes sense that marriage should be a place where two people truly listen to and help each other name their experiences. That's why we get attracted to each other in the first place, because we meet someone who is interested in understanding our deeper feelings, intuitions, and experiences. Marriage is also a place where the two of you know that you belong, that you count, and that you can turn to each other for support, care and comfort. And empathy is the skill that lets you provide meaning attribution and caring to your spouse.

Empathy demonstrates to the other person that meaning attribution and caring are high on your list. When we empathize with someone we can say "I know what you mean" by paraphrasing or restating to that person what we just heard. We communicate that we care for our spouse by trying to express the feeling we hear. While we can never know exactly how another feels, we can come closer to understanding by saying things like, "It sounds like you're feeling . . . about. . . ."

Another way we approximate the feelings of another's state is by modeling that state in our own bodies. So if your spouse is down your own expressions might appear down in order for you to communicate that you understand what he or she is going through. One of the best examples of this bodily form of empathy, though not intentional, is when a husband gains weight along with his pregnant wife, saying to her in effect, "While I can't appreciate totally what you're going through I am trying to approximate in my own body the changes I see happen in yours."

A Slice of Life

Sean sat before the marriage counselor, perplexed and stressed out. He and his wife Shelly have been married for eleven years and prior to that had lived with each other right after graduating from high school. What he didn't understand is that just recently his wife told him that she wasn't sure that she loved him anymore and that she felt that he tried to control her. As the therapist led him through an initial assessment Sean confided that in the beginning of their relationship he served as Shelly's "protector"; she had come from a physically abusive family and had a low self-esteem. Sean would bolster her confidence in the early years. But as time went on Shelly became more confident and didn't need as much protection and bolstering. And Sean's role of the protector began to shift. He became more afraid of losing Shelly and sometimes responded with anger and sometimes with jealousy when Shelly would act independently of him. Shelly told him just recently that she was afraid of his anger and that she felt controlled by it. She also entered private therapy to sort through her own feelings.

Sean and his therapist constructed an initial plan. He would work on expressing his anger in a more appropriate manner where Shelly could feel secure and safe. Additionally, he would work on his own lack of confidence and jealousy and intensity that Shelly saw as controlling. He would also try to give Shelly both time and emotional space in which to sort through her issues.

He wanted to get into marriage counseling with Shelly but realized that this would have to wait until she was ready. In the meantime the decision for him was whether he was ready to work on his own issues.

AWARENESS IN ACTION

Sometimes we harm the foundations of our marriage unintentionally through our attitudes and/or behaviors. The important thing here is for each of you to be able to speak your mind honestly and respectfully if this is happening. It's far better to voice your concerns earlier than later. In the above case it might be too late for Sean to change, especially if Shelly doesn't want to participate with him in making the necessary changes.

- Do you think there is any hope for Sean in the above slice of life?
- Is it possible that being a "protector" of Shelly also had a darker side, one where he became controlling?

- Are the core marital conditions alive and well in your marriage?
- Are you aware of times in your own marriage where the two of you had to clarify and focus on the core conditions?
- What has been your biggest challenge to date concerning these conditions?

THE SPIRITUAL DIMENSION: EMPATHY IN ACTION

St. Paul wrote about the "self-emptying" of Christ: "Though he was in the form of God [he] did not regard equality with God something to be grasped. Rather, he emptied himself . . . coming in human likeness" (Phil 2: 6-7).

Marriage often mirrors the action of Christ in that there is a similar "self emptying" process often required of spouses. We know that we are equal to each other, yet we often empty ourselves of our own needs to put the needs of the other first. We do this because of love, because of empathy for the other, whether the other is our spouse or our child.

Justice demands that the other acknowledge our equality and rights to get our needs met. Empathy encourages us not to cling to our needs in an immature grasping. Empathy moves us out of our own ego state and into the state of the other. When we say to our spouse, "I see what you mean" or "You must feel . . ." we go through a self-emptying similar to what

Christ modeled. When we don't feel listened to by our spouse then the demands of justice begin to take over. Sometimes both spouses can get into a war of hurt where they compare how much they have been hurt by the other. Empathy moves our hearts to consider the hurt of the other. It encourages us to take the risk of vulnerability.

Answer Honestly then Share....

Trusting others is for me...

One way you can respect me is...

My strengths are....

13

CLARIFYING YOUR EXPECTATIONS

Don't marry a man to reform him—that's what reform schools are for.
—MAE WEST

To accomplish anything well we need great expectations. Expectations are created by our imaginations, they represent the outcome we are hoping for. The Olympic athlete imagines herself performing flawlessly, thus creating a positive self-expectation for the event. Without expectations we could not anticipate the future, and if our expectations are low, the future will look very bleak.

This chapter explores how we can talk about and create appropriate expectations. Before you were married you were probably told by many people that you had unrealistic expectations concerning marriage. Others told you, perhaps, that you should lower your expectation, as if marriage was an oversold commodity that wasn't worth the price. Now that you've been married for a while you have probably discovered the problem with low expectations: if you don't expect much you won't get much. Lowering your expectations only encourages you to expect less out of your marriage.

Instead, why not put the emphasis on adjusting your expectations to meet the reality of your own lived situation. This includes your own personal expectations of yourself, your work, your children, and the expectations you have of each other. Adjusting expectations involves checking in with each other and checking out your expectations. It involves some dialog and conversation.

Let's examine seven areas where married people can get themselves stuck and experience problems. Difficulties in these areas can bog you down and make you question the quality of your marriage.

1. Expectations About Your Relationship

Some common expectations go like this: As a married couple we'll be best friends. We'll do everything together. We will share our innermost thoughts. There will be no secrets. We won't get bored with each other.

When our expectations aren't met, we sometimes say to our spouse: "I thought you were my friend but . . . we're not spending much time together, we're not sharing deeply anymore, and we're fighting more." The reality of marriage often calls us to adjust our expectations. Friendships get strained and pulled in many directions. And you have all that stress to contend with: your job, your kids and their busy schedules, not to mention any unexpected developments like a health emergency.

2. Expectations About Being Lovers

Here we think: We'll make love frequently and passionately. We will be spontaneous. We will agree on the frequency of sex. We won't refuse each other. Because we are spontaneous we won't have to plan to make love.

When our expectations meet the reality of life we might think or say to our spouse: We used to be so passionate in our lovemaking, but now we don't connect with each other sexually like we used to. I wonder if you love me like you used to.

The reality of married life—especially when children come—can challenge the spontaneity and passion of lovemaking. But it doesn't mean that you have to continually lower your expectations. It means that you have to talk to one another respectfully about your expectations and needs. A complicating factor here is that you need to realize that the two of you respond to stress and tension differently. Women tend to want to be emotionally connected with their spouses before lovemaking. If there is a lot of stress then this could make it more difficult for the two of you to connect sexually. This is especially true if there is tension. For many women talking about problems with their spouse precedes lovemaking because they feel more emotionally connected. Men sometimes find it easier to put tension aside and make love to their wives. This can create confusion with women because they see their men putting off talking about tension in the relationship in favor of lovemaking. This can lead to a sense of being used. Many men see lovemaking as a way of becoming emotionally connected; this is often the opposite response to how women see lovemaking.

3. Expectations Concerning Roles and Responsibilities

Another source of tension between a couple has to do with expectations concerning roles and responsibilities. The peril of not clarifying roles and responsibilities in a marriage can certainly lead you to feel that you are stuck in a role you would rather change.

As a married couple you are partners in time. Your roles and responsibilities will shift and change as you go through transitions together. When there is tension over who does what, when, and the amount of time spent together, you might say to your spouse, "I thought we had a deal about household chores, but now I'm finding that I'm doing most of what you agreed to do and I'm feeling taken advantage of." Perhaps the general agreement you had in your early marriage has begun to break down as your children have come along. It's best to remember that every major transition will require some checking in with each other and renegotiating of the issues involved. You may still arrive at the same conclusions but now they are the result of checking in with each other and clarifying your positions. Otherwise, resentment can begin to build.

4. Expectations About Parenting

Parenting can bring out both the best and the worst in us. When we parent well, we get in touch with the loving nurturing side of ourselves. But we sometimes encounter habits and tendencies about ourselves that we didn't know were present. For instance, as your children grow older, you might find yourself being short and impatient, something you never expected. Then there is the issue of how to share parenting tasks, who does what for the children: gives them their baths, feeds them, shops for them, spends time with them.

Resentment can arise if one of you feels that the parenting load is unequally shared or if there are disagreements in how to communicate with and discipline children. Another typical pattern that causes tension has one parent—usually the husband—playing the role of the playful funny clown with the children while the other spouse is the disciplinarian and rule enforcer.

5. Happiness Expectations

Happiness expectations build on relationship and role expectations. Certainly if there are unresolved tensions in these two areas, your happiness will be lessened. But this area also has to do with your own specific happiness. Do you enjoy what you are doing, whether you are working outside the home or inside? What gives you satisfaction? What are your expectations concerning careers? Included in this set of expectations are both of your expectations about how to make decisions concerning a career path. This can be quite tricky, especially if there are hidden or unvoiced expectations about who will sacrifice for the other.

We all have a lot to be concerned about and sometimes we look to our spouse to take away our worries. Job change, loss, major illness, death of a family member, or a move to another geographical area are just a few examples of the stressful things that can happen to us. Even the birth of children, while a happy event, can create tough times for a couple and result in a change in sleep patterns, schedules, and the like.

When our expectations about how the other should be there for us aren't met we may say something like this: You said you would hang in there with me but I feel alone and abandoned.

You said you would help out, but I'm carrying all the load. We want our spouses generally to "be there for us" and get hurt when this doesn't happen. Sometimes, however, we fail to adequately check out these expectations with our spouse. Remember, in times of high stress and pain it's instinctive to retreat into ourselves, to develop unrealistic expectations about how the other can care for us.

Most important, however, is the belief about happiness. Many married people believe that it is their job to make the other person happy. If you have this belief it will eventually cause you grief and bewilderment, because you cannot make your spouse happy unless he or she makes a choice to move into a higher state of satisfaction or happiness. Your job in your marriage is to listen to what makes your spouse happy and then decide if you can help him or her attain happiness. Changing your belief about happiness allows you to place the responsibility for stating what makes you happy on your shoulders as opposed to your spouse's. This means, among other things, that you will need to tell your spouse how you feel and what really interests you. It also means that you will need to really listen to what your spouse tells you about his or her happiness.

6. Expectations About Conflict

Another area of expectations has to do with how we handle conflict. As we noted in the last chapter, many of us are afraid of conflict and would just rather not deal with it. Even if we say we will face conflict with our spouse we often have unconscious, gut level responses that make it hard to do what we say we will do. So it's possible that one or both of you, even though you have verbally promised not to avoid conflict, puts off dealing with difficult things with your spouse. If this is happening the tension in your relationship will begin to escalate. It's a paradox that the avoiding of conflict actually increases marital conflict over time.

Many people believe that conflict is toxic and dangerous. If you believe this you'll probably try to avoid conflict because you expect it to damage you and the relationship. The most important thing here is for the two of you to examine your beliefs and responses to conflict so that you can resolve conflict more successfully. The most damaging thing you can do is to get into a consistent pattern of avoiding conflict with your spouse.

7. Expectations Concerning Money and Finance

Financial trouble in a marriage can be highly stressful. Marriage and family life involve many financial responsibilities, and each of you brings a set of beliefs about saving and spending money to your marriage. One of you might be a "saver," the other a "spender." One of you might want to make "safe" financial investments while the other wants to take more risks. Money, and the lack of it, has a way of defining our priorities. Chances are that both of you have some differences regarding money and you have both had to compromise. Perhaps each of you has learned something from the other regarding finances and spending. The most important thing is to recognize and discuss your areas of agreement as well as difference.

STRATEGIES TO CLARIFY EXPECTATIONS

Unclear expectations can create a good deal of conflict in a marriage. Since the two of you know each other well, it's always a good rule to surface your expectations and to talk about them when you can. The following are a few suggestions for doing just that.

1. Make the unconscious conscious. Listen to what is going on in your gut, your instinct. If something feels out of balance then share that with your spouse in a way that is respectful.
2. Check in with each other and check out your mutual expectations. Name what you want or expect in the areas of friendship, emotional support, household chores, sexual intimacy, and parenting. Listen to your spouse's needs.

3. Be ready to clarify expectations during times of transition. Also, be ready to renegotiate specific role expectations.

4. Don't ignore resentment. When you begin to feel resentment this is a sign that something is out of balance. Commit to facing this with your spouse. Don't avoid, but talk respectfully about what is going on.

5. Take responsibility for your behavior. Sometimes a previously unseen aspect of your personality will be displayed to your spouse. For instance, you may not have had a problem with anger, but now you do. Are you prepared to explore if any of this is caused by unresolved family of origin issues?

6. Work together on parenting. If your expectations differ consider taking a parenting class at your local church or school so that both of you create common expectations.

7. Clarify and talk to your spouse about your own personal happiness. Share your expectations concerning your career, how you see yourself, and if you are happy with yourself. Be ready to change your belief if you think it's your job to make your spouse happy. Be ready to talk with your spouse about what makes you happy and what you want out of life.

8. Examine your belief about conflict. Talk about whether conflict scares you and whether you avoid conflict. Above

all, commit to facing conflict with your spouse. If there is something about the way you work through conflict together that you find disrespectful or not helpful, talk about it. Agree to seek professional help if the two of you cannot fix this yourself. Your relationship is worth it.

A Slice of Life

Tony and Jennifer have been married for ten years. Tony is the youngest of three children and he came from a family where his father was a perfectionist and held the children to very high standards. Growing up Tony was afraid of his father's anger, especially when he didn't achieve according to his father's standards. Tony learned at an early age that sometimes it was easier for him to fudge a bit on the truth. He found out that he could avoid his father's wrath if he stretched the truth a bit or just out and out lied to him.

This pattern of stretching the truth and sometimes lying stayed with Tony through his high school and college days. When he met Jennifer he was attracted to her energy and forthrightness. Their marriage was happy, but there was one thing that he didn't tell Jennifer, one crucial fact about himself: he didn't really graduate from college. He was three credit hours short and decided to "walk" through graduation exercises, telling his friends and family that he in fact had graduated. And he later forgot about making up the three credits.

When his employer found out that he never got a degree, he threatened to fire him for misrepresenting his background. With his work world crashing down on him he decided to confide in Jennifer. "I was afraid if you knew the truth you would get mad at me and criticize me," Tony told Jennifer. This was news to Jennifer, who only wanted to understand better why her husband didn't trust her to know the truth. After talking about this Jennifer realized that Tony brought a sensitivity to criticism into his marriage along with a fear of conflict. Tony reassured her that he would be truthful from then on. For her part Jennifer was reassured to a degree, but worried that the same pattern would reassert itself later on in their marriage.

AWARENESS IN ACTION

Expectations, when left unstated, can create a great deal of tension in your relationship. Sometimes we even expect the other to know what we are thinking or feeling and get angry when our spouse doesn't respond the way we want.

- Do the two of you ever engage in a process of mind reading?
- How easy is it for you to say what you want or how you feel? Were you allowed to

have a voice concerning your feelings, thoughts, and expectations when you were growing up?

- What expectations have you had to adjust since you have been married?
- In the above case Tony tried to keep the peace no matter what the consequences were for him. Have you ever become stuck or troubled because of a belief that it was your job to make people happy?
- Do you agree that clarifying your own expectations with your spouse could improve your relationship?

THE SPIRITUAL DIMENSION: HAPPINESS AND SATISFACTION EXPECTATIONS

Does God want you to be happy in your marriage? At first glance that's an easy answer. Of course God wants you to be happy. But what's the balance between achieving your own personal happiness and your spouse's personal happiness? Sometimes your interests and expectations collide and there is conflict between the two of you. And you may even compete to get your needs and expectations met, and get angry with the other for placing his/her needs and expectations over yours. And what makes you happy anyway? Is it in getting stuff for yourself, giving things and money, achieving your own personal goals, helping others reach their potential? Maybe we are the happiest when there is a balance between self fulfillment and encouragement of the other. The prayer of St. Francis says, "it is in giving that we receive." Achieving this balance means that we make the commitment to discern the right path for ourselves and our loved ones.

Answer Honestly then Share....

What I want from you when we are tense is...

Right now I feel...... Happy sad angry fearful anxious joyful tense frustrated...(name the feeling)

And I can take responsibility for that by doing.... (say what you will do)

14

BEING OPEN TO CHANGE

After marriage, all things
change. And one of them
better be you.
—ELIZABETH HAWES

In the movie As Good As It Gets Jack Nicholson plays a querulous writer who suffers from obsessive compulsive disorder (OCD). He meets a waitress played by Helen Hunt and gradually develops a relationship with her. He quickly discovers that he is attracted to her balanced, even personality and falls in love with her. As a result of his falling in love he decides to go back on medication to control his OCD. And at the climax of the movie, when his relationship with her hangs in the balance he says to her, "Knowing you has made me want to be a better man."

This is a great summary of what marriage is all about. In the best moments of our marriage we can say to our spouse, "Knowing you makes me want to be a better person." The desire to be a better person brings us to the crossroads of change, and to take responsibility for how we want to change.

One of the toughest transitions any married person goes through is the transition from asking your spouse to change to accepting responsibility to change yourself. Obviously it's easier if the other person changes. But the request for change that we make of our spouse often resides on an unconscious or semi-conscious level. We can easily fall into a power struggle with our spouse over how things are done, which habits are found distasteful, and which needs aren't met. You may even struggle with the reasons why you're having power struggles!

WE GROW ON OUR DIFFERENCES

One reason the request for change causes problems has to do with how the two of you met each other and fell in love. There is a saying in the marriage therapy field: "We meet on what we share in common, we grow on our differences." In the beginning, when you fell in love with each other, you probably experienced a large area of common feelings, values, and interests. You may even have learned new ways of doing things from each other, and new interests as well. When you look back on this period, you will probably discover a lot of good will toward sharing common interests and values. Concerning the differences you had at the time, you both were probably optimistic that you could compromise. Indeed, you may have enjoyed a good track record at resolving your differences. And it makes sense that your ability to compromise and tolerate differences should carry into your marriage. Why then are you arguing more and compromising less?

As we settle into marriage more of our hidden self emerges. It's not that we intentionally hide things from our spouse; sometimes we even hide them from ourselves. For instance, someone who comes from a family where one or both parents expressed a good deal of anger may decide to adopt a more "laid back" approach toward conflict. His or her fiancé may be attracted to this calm approach. But, as the marriage unfolds, what a surprise it is to find that this person sometimes has a difficulty with anger, just as one of his or her parents did. This "hidden" aspect to the personality emerges over time in the marriage. There are many "hidden" parts to us that can create surprise in our relationships.

Whenever a change occurs, hidden aspects of ourselves can surface. The birth of a child, a move, a job change, indeed any stressful situation can bring something previously unseen to the surface.

Another reason this happens is the very safety of marriage. Because we trust our spouse to be there and remain faithful to our marriage commitment, we feel freer to "tell things like they are." We can speak our mind more freely or do things more freely.

Nevertheless, when differences emerge in a relationship it can be a time of real tension, but also real growth. Maybe there is something built into our genetic structure that encourages us to see differences as a threat. Perhaps we secretly fear that if our spouse is truly different in some way he or she will stop loving us and leave us for someone more like them.

The crisis that a couple faces when serious differences emerge can be voiced one of two ways. The first way says, "I don't understand why you think and feel differently from me. If you were only more like me, things would be different." The second way says, "I sometimes get a bit exasperated and maybe a little afraid that we have different ways of thinking and feeling, but I want to appreciate that we're different and try to understand our differences in a way that enhances our relationship. I don't want to see differences as bad."

DEALING WITH DIFFERENCES

The following points might help you grow on your differences and negotiate the change you want in your relationship.

- There are differences in temperament that can sometimes cause problems if not understood properly. One of you might be more spontaneous, the other more structured; one of you might be a thinker, the other a feeler; one might be more physically expressive, the other might be more reserved. Allow yourself to think of these differences in a neutral way.

- There are also differences in the way people solve conflict. One of you might be more at ease with conflict, the other might tend to avoid it. Don't spend time wishing the other would change. Rather talk about your own approach, and commit to negotiating a style that respects each of your approaches. You might have to get into marriage counseling to do this negotiating, especially if the two of you feel especially stuck.

- Give up trying to change the other. People only change and do something different when they are ready to. You are allowed to say what you want and what would make things more helpful to you, but pouting and getting angry with your spouse for not doing things your way will only make matters worse. When you give up trying to change your spouse, it begins to free your spouse to take more responsibility. This is because the two of you are not in a "push-pull" power struggle characterized by stubbornness and resistance.

- Know your own bottom line non-negotiable values like respect, honesty, trust, etc. If any of your spouse's behaviors violate these values, this is a signal to get into marriage counseling. You do not have to put up with behaviors that violate your bottom line values. For instance, if you're married to someone who abuses alcohol, you can't make your spouse stop, but you can refuse to ride in the car when she or he is drinking. And you can attend an Al-Anon group.

- On behaviors that don't violate your bottom line non-negotiable values: keep your focus on the behaviors, don't attack the person. Tell your spouse about the particular personality traits that you are striving to accept. Ask your spouse to discuss this with you, and if you need outside help, get it.

- Take responsibility for how you want to change. This is scary. It keeps the focus on your behaviors. Your behaviors are in the circle of your control. For instance, if you're not happy with your life and have been subtly blaming your spouse for this, start thinking about what you can do to achieve greater personal happiness.

- Talk together about the changes you want to make, personally and in your relationship. Speak for yourself, not for the other. Create a plan if you can. Encourage each other, but don't demand.

BLOCKS TO CHANGE

Have you ever had the experience of attempting to change something in your life yet found that you couldn't quite get the job done? Why is it that change is sometimes so difficult? Below are some reasons why we sometimes find ourselves blocked when we face changing something about ourselves. The following represent reasons why change is so difficult. Identify the ones holding you back from making the change you want.

Fear

We're often afraid of trying something new, either because we are not confident or because of our past experiences. Fear can keep us chained to old behaviors that are unhealthy and even harmful.

Negative Self-Talk

Have you noticed how sometimes we tell ourselves we are either not good enough, not smart enough, or not attractive enough? We give ourselves hundreds of messages every day. These messages reinforce a pattern of behavior. Negative self-talk usually leads to self-defeating behaviors.

Lack of Consistent Encouragement

Child experts tell us that in order for a child to have positive self esteem, he/she needs to hear five positive comments for every negative comment. The same ratio holds for adults.

Cost of Change Is Perceived as Too Great to Offset the Gain of Change.

Every significant change involves a cost or loss and a possible gain. A person who gets married, for instance gives up the single life for the gain of marital intimacy. Another person might want to quit smoking but not want to give up the pleasure of it. In order to really change we must be convinced that the benefits will be greater than the cost.

Lack of Options

Sometimes we want to change but don't know that we can. We might feel that we are destined to remain in a state of unhappiness because we simply don't know that there are options available to us.

Complaining Is Easier Than Changing

It's a lot easier to complain about one's lot in life than to do something about it. Change takes a conscious decision and requires work on our part.

CAN YOU REALLY CHANGE?

Change can be both fearful and exhilarating, but to change we must overcome our built-in tendency toward habit. We often just do things because we're used to the pattern. Our brains form neural pathways that become reflexive. Changing the neural pattern takes time, but not as much time as you think. Below are some suggestions that might help in creating the change we want to see happen in our lives.

- Know what you want. A well-formed outcome that states the behaviors you want to change and the new behaviors you want to adopt. Example: "I want to control my temper and be more relaxed."
- Change your self-talk. We are continually giving ourselves messages about what we want, who we are, and how we feel about ourselves. Become aware of how you talk to yourself and change the negatives to positives.
- Find someone who can act as a coach or mentor. Finding the right person to give encouragement and give suggestions on specific strategies is very important. This could be your spouse, but be clear as to what you're are asking for.
- Imagine yourself adopting the change you want. See yourself completing the

change. What will be different about you once you successfully adopt the change?

- Identify the new behaviors that can substitute for the old behaviors. Be as specific as you can. Many people give up because they don't get specific enough.

- Create either a Personal Plan, a Relationship Plan, or a Career Plan. State your goal or outcome, how you want to change on both the belief and behavior level, and how you are going to get there.

A Slice of Life

Scott and Cindy's marriage of fourteen years was at the point of breaking up. Scott had suddenly announced that he was leaving and told Cindy that he "couldn't take it anymore." This was a surprise to her and she pleaded with him to get into some form of marriage counseling with her.

During the marriage counseling it finally came out that Scott never liked the fact that when they argued Cindy would raise her voice and yell at him. He would become quiet at times and leave the room, only to have Cindy become more vocal and pursue him. Cindy was surprised that her yelling had such a negative effect on him. She had come from a very expressive family where verbal arguments and raised voices were just a normal part of her life.

Scott also felt that Cindy would become critical of him when he would spontaneously announce that he had plans for their weekend. At times it would seem that Cindy would resist every one of his suggestions. What Scott didn't understand was that Cindy was the type of person who wanted to plan ahead. She tended to be more organized and liked to talk about weekend plans in advance. Cindy also got frustrated and angry with Scott when he sprung activities on her. To her it seemed disrespectful. That's when the yelling began. Scott had consistently felt criticized yet he admitted to not making much of an attempt to talk to her about his negative reaction to the way they argued and the way they planned.

Both of them became aware that they spent a lot of time wishing that the other would change and that there had been a long simmering power struggle between them. They both agreed that each of them could take responsibility to change certain specific things, that Cindy could work on arguing without yelling and Scott could work on becoming more direct with Cindy about what he wanted and communicating with her more. Both also realized that there were acceptance issues as well that each needed to work on. And both wondered if too much damage had already been inflicted on their relationship.

Awareness in Action

We are often used to getting what we want. Sometimes we take a consumer attitude toward our significant relationships and think of our spouse as a complaint department. We think to ourselves, "if only you would change or do it my way things would be so much better." In the above case Scott didn't stick up for himself and perhaps had some wishful thinking about Cindy's changing her behavior. Eventually he had to face whether it was worth his changing by speaking his mind more clearly to Cindy.

- Do you think there have been times when the two of you have fought over change and who will change?
- Does it make sense that accepting your spouse and changing yourself is the better way, even though it is more difficult?
- What, if anything, is blocking you from making the changes you want?
- Are there any negative messages you give yourself? What are they?
- Can you identify any new behaviors you want to adopt? Can you identify any new beliefs about yourself that you want to adopt?

- Who can serve as a coach and help you identify the changes you want to make?

THE SPIRITUAL DIMENSION: A PRAYER FOR SERENITY

It is perhaps best known as the Serenity Prayer, having been adopted by twelve step groups as a common prayer which expresses the desire for change. It is also a great prayer for married couples.

God,

> grant me serenity to accept the things I cannot change,
> the courage to change the things I can
> and the wisdom to know the difference,
> living one day at a time,
> enjoying one moment at a time,
> accepting hardship as a pathway to peace,
> taking, as Jesus did, this sinful world as it is,
> not as I would have it,
> trusting that you will make all things right
> if I surrender to your will,
> so that I may be reasonably happy in this life
> and supremely happy with you forever in the next.

—Reinhold Neibuhr

Answer Honestly then Share....

I can help you meet your needs by...

You can help me meet my needs by...

Today I want....

15

TAKING CARE OF YOURSELF AND YOUR SPOUSE

Do what you can, with what you have,
where you are.
— THEODORE ROOSEVELT

It might seem strange to suggest that an important strategy for insuring the success of your marriage has to do with a commitment on your part to take care of yourself over the course of your marriage. It's a fact, however, that many spouses spend more time worrying about their partners than themselves, to say nothing about the worry over children.

The other side of worry is wellness. Marriage, when it's working right, can be seen as a community of wellness, where each of you actively seeks to be well and encourages the other to seek wellness. When it comes to taking care of yourself, the following go into a comprehensive list of factors that comprise wellness. These factors, when applied to your relationship, have the potential to increase both your personal and marital satisfaction. This list is presented to you and your spouse in the hopes it will enable you to have a more comprehensive conversation about how each of you takes care of yourself. Wellness is a sense of balance and well being which comes from integrating the many diverse but interconnected parts of the self. Wellness consists of the interaction of the following parts of our lives:

Sense of Well Being:
Physical self
Spirituality
Emotional self
Connectedness
Sense of humor
Sense of hope in future
Relational self
Work self

Physical Self:

This part of the self comprises our body image, how we feel about our bodies, whether we feel fit, overweight, too thin. The question here is, are you comfortable in your own skin? This sense of physical self comes to us in part from what we were taught about our bodies by our own families and in part by our own genetic heritage. Ask yourself honestly: Do you feel good about how you are taking care of your physical self? Do you get enough exercise? When under stress do you sometimes harm your body by either drinking or eating too much? Do you consume too much caffeine? What could you be doing differently to take care of yourself in this area?

Work Self:

This part of the self has to do with how you interact with others at work, whether you are happy with your work and have a sense of direction to your career. Do you feel trapped by your job, do you find yourself complaining about your work? Does your work give you energy or take energy from you? If you feel stuck what, if anything can you do differently to start feeling unstuck?

Relational Self:

This is the part of the self that has to do with how you are in relationship with the significant people in your life, your spouse, your children, co-workers, friends and other family members. Do you feel connected to these people? Is your relationship with your spouse energy-producing or energy-sapping? With your children, energy-producing or energy-sapping? What can you do to show the ones who care about you that you want to improve on the relationship you have right now with them?

Emotional Self:

This is the part of the self that has to do with how we feel about ourselves and the world on a daily basis. This part of the self is affected by our own family background, our genetic makeup and also by the amount of stress that we find ourselves under. This is also the part of ourselves that has to do with reaching out and developing friendships with others. But sometimes we are just too busy to take care of our emotional selves and we fail to recognize the signs of burnout, depression, or anxiety. Do you take the time to adequately relieve your stress in a healthy way through exercise and leisure? If you are slightly burnt out or depressed do you allow your spouse to raise this issue with you or do you get defensive and refuse to think about it? What positive steps can you take to improve upon your own mental health?

The Spiritual Self:

This addresses the part of the self that asks the bigger questions of where we came from, how did it all begin, is there a God who cares about you. This is the sense of self that struggles with the tough questions, like why do good people suffer. It's also the part of the self that sees a deeper meaning in making connections among one's various endeavors.

These connections can be found through the practice of religion, but they can also be found in work with the poor, the environment, or the many other good causes that exist today. Through the spiritual sense of self one asks the deeper questions about good and evil, values and your place in the scheme of things. Do you feel connected to the larger issues? Are there organizations or causes outside your own marriage and family that draw your attention and give value and meaning to your life?

The Playful Self:

This addresses the part of the self that wants to play and relax, to unwind, to relieve stress, and to transcend the problems of life that always seem to be ready to pounce on us. Laughing releases endorphins and allows us to rejuvenate ourselves. Why do children have the capacity to laugh, cut loose, play, have fun, while we adults struggle just to enjoy a little part of our day? Children are not usually beset with all the concerns of life as you are. Do you have a laughter and leisure deficit? Are you working too long, getting less ahead, and not having any fun? Has your own life, maybe even your relationship with your spouse gone a little stale? What can you do to add some fun to your life? What can the two of you do together to have fun and enjoy your life?

Through the Years

Okay, you're probably sold on the idea of wellness. After all, who can be against wellness? But as you get older you will begin to understand that, if you want to be as healthy as possible, you need to attend to these factors. Gradually—and sometimes not too gradually—we age and there will come a time when we face the limits of life. All of us will die one day, no matter how much we follow our culture's denial of death. But do we want to face getting older in a way that emphasizes health and wellness, actively striving to take care of ourselves? Think of it this way: if we neglect our bodily and emotional well being most likely we will have more illnesses in our lives and feel more depressed about ourselves. And it's possible that as we get older we will find ourselves more limited by the impact of not taking care of ourselves. Wellness is not a way of denying the inevitability of death, it's a way of understanding ourselves as persons who realize the limit imposed by death. That's why spirituality is a big part of wellness; the limit of death forces us to ask the bigger questions concerning life after death and God.

The paradox of wellness is that you cannot force your spouse to take care of him or herself. Try as you like if your spouse refuses to watch his or her cholesterol and weight there is little you can do to force the issue. The same is true of something like smoking; you can limit smoking to only the outdoors and you can tell your spouse how unhappy you are about it but unless your spouse truly decides to quit, this will probably be a losing battle for you.

FOUR VITAL QUESTIONS

There are four vital questions that each of us can ask our partner about health and wellness:

1. How do you feel about yourself?

This is a question we can ask frequently. How do you feel about yourself physically, emotionally, relationally? To really ask the question out of concern for the other and to really listen to their response is an act of love. How do you feel, really? This is a good question to ask of each other on a regular basis because it indicates that you really care for each other.

2. How do you take care of yourself?

This is another vital question that puts the responsibility for taking care of self on the shoulders of the individual. You are the only person who knows what it feels like to be in your skin. No one else knows that experience like you do. You know best what you need in order to take care of yourself. That is why your spouse asks how you're doing, how you're taking care of yourself. Sometimes you might want to fault your spouse for not taking care of you, and sometimes your spouse might be insensitive to your needs. But the responsibility for stating how you're to be cared for starts with you.

3. What do you want for yourself, from me?

In the areas of wellness outlined above the question of want becomes very specific. What do you want for yourself physically, emotionally, spiritually, etc? To ask this question means that your spouse really cares how you are doing emotionally, physically, spiritually, relationally. To ask this question means that the two of you might have to take some time to talk all this through. Also, in speaking of what you want for yourself you might also uncover something that you want your spouse to consider doing. If you make the request realize that it has to be delivered freely, meaning that your spouse might suggest a modification or might not be able to do what you want exactly the way you want it.

4. How can I help you take care of yourself?

While each of us has to realize that we cannot do it all, there are ways we can help. For instance, suppose that your spouse wants to quit smoking. Your question then becomes, "How can I help you? Is there anything I can do?" Asking it this way might help you avoid nagging, demanding, and criticizing if your spouse doesn't always follow through on the commitment.

A Word About Alcohol and Substance Abuse

How we take care of ourselves and handle the stress of life is an important decision for all of us. It's no surprise that people often turn to alcohol and other substances to help them unwind. Alcohol still remains the drug of choice for the majority of citizens in the United States. Certainly, it's okay to have a drink. Part of the problem is that ninety percent of people who become addicted to a drug are not aware that they are crossing the line from occasional use to addictive use.

What are some of the signs that you might be crossing that line? Looking forward to your next drink, drinking to relieve stress and tension, an increase in consumption, the subject of drinking becomes a source of tension at home, and a decrease in work performance due to drinking or another substance are major indicators. The key question is: Are you in control of the substance or is it in control of you? For instance, can you go out with friends or to a party and not drink at all and have fun? If not, then maybe the substance is more in control of you than you realize.

A Slice of Life

Connie and Mike have been married for nineteen years. They have two teens, ages sixteen and fourteen. Both Connie and Mike have taken relatively good care of themselves through the years, although both of them have struggled a bit with weight gain. When Connie was forty-two she entered menopause; this development caught both of them off guard. Before menopause she began having irregular menstrual cycles. As this process developed Connie experienced mood swings, hot flashes, muscle pain, and she also began to gain more weight. She knew that she was experiencing a mild form of depression as a result of this transition, especially since it came years before she was expecting it.

Mike, of course, was affected by the impact of menopause and often felt helpless. He wasn't sure how to support her on questions such as estrogen replacement therapy. Mike was also concerned about Connie's depression and was worried about her weight gain, but he was reluctant to talk about this because he feared she would be defensive. Both of them struggled with the transition, each from their own perspectives.

Connie's doctor gave her permission to grieve and face the transition ahead of her. She gave Connie valuable information concerning estrogen replacement therapy and invited her and Mike to discuss together the options that Connie had. She also framed the transition in a positive light and emphasized with Connie the importance of eating well and getting regular exercise. As a result Connie began to develop a plan that included diet changes and more regular exercise. She also became more clear with Mike about how he could support her and what she needed from him as she moved through this transition.

Mike also faced his own reactions to this transition. He had not anticipated that Connie would enter menopause so early. He was in good shape, athletic and worked out regularly. During this transition he became acutely aware of how much he valued physical activity and sexual contact with Connie. He saw her struggle with mood swings, depression, and weight gain and he tried as best he could to be supportive. He was determined to be positive but was also afraid to share with her any of his own reaction for fear that she would become more depressed and defensive.

AWARENESS IN ACTION

Stress is a part of daily living, yet we sometimes desensitize ourselves to its impact on us. We work hard, sometimes very long hours. And we sometimes forget that we have all those different and good parts to ourselves.

- How well do you take care of yourself? Do you have concerns about the way

your spouse takes care of him or herself?
Can you discuss these concerns with your
spouse in a non-defensive and caring
manner?

- Are there any areas of wellness listed
  above where you could be doing a
  better job taking care of yourself?
- What action can you take to feel better
  about yourself?

THE SPIRITUAL DIMENSION: WHOLENESS IS HOLINESS

This phrase sums up the idea that the quest for
holiness is a holistic endeavor involving all parts
of the human person: the thinking, feeling,
physical, psychological, and sexual parts of
who we are, as well as how we were formed
in our own families of origin. To be holy, to be
whole, is to be well at its most fundamental
level.

There is a paradox to being well, to being
whole, in that in order to truly be whole we
have to be open to moving through pain and
brokenness toward healing. To be open to
love is to be open to having our heart broken.
Not allowing our hearts to take this risk means
shutting ourselves off from the risk of love. This
isn't being whole, it's being scared and afraid.

But to be whole means that we take the risk
of love and life, and face our pain, not run from
it or seek to avoid it by self-medicating with
alcohol or other drugs. If you are to be a whole

person you have to embrace the fragmented parts of your life; some of these parts you are sometimes not too proud of. They represent the unfinished business of your life's journey and they cry out for integration.

Being open to the God-force in your life means being open to pain, but also to healing. A man who was about to die from a terrible cancer, told a minister who visited him right before he died, "Even though I'm dying, I've been made whole." He had reached the wholeness that lies beyond pain and suffering.

Answer Honestly then Share....

Five things I do to relieve my stress are...

Today my stress level is at (1 to 5)

When I get stressed I want....

16

PRACTICING THE ART OF FORGIVENESS

The weak can never forgive.
Forgiveness is the attribute of
the strong.
– MOHANDAS GANDHI

A mature marriage is built on spouses respecting and building the core conditions that create a solid relationship. But there comes a time in most relationships where the core conditions of trust, respect, honesty and fidelity will be threatened or even violated. And that brings your marriage to the reality of forgiveness. Even the little assaults to the core conditions, like forgetting to call home to say you'll be late, require to some extent the ability to seek and grant forgiveness.

Forgiveness is an art that takes practice and some discipline. It's also like eating your vegetables. You know that they are good for you and will keep you healthy long term; so you discipline yourself by eating the carrots knowing that in the long run you'll be all the more healthy and happy. While forgiveness is sometimes hard to swallow, it will keep your marital system healthy and intact through the years.

What Is Forgiveness?

In its simplest form forgiveness is the cancellation of a debt that someone owes you, whether that debt is monetary or emotional. Frederick DeBlasio, therapist and social worker at the University of Maryland, says that forgiveness is a "letting go of resentments, bitterness, and negative thinking toward someone" (Counseling Today, May 2000). This definition implies that someone whom you thought of as an equal has done some action that has deprived you of something of great value; that "something" can be money, bodily well being, mental health, trust, self-esteem, or much more. The perpetrator's action makes you feel resentment and hurt, and causes negative thoughts toward that person. So if your spouse has lied to you not only will you feel hurt and resentment, you will most likely think badly of your spouse. And this negative thinking ("my spouse is a liar, I can't trust him or her") will begin to shape your future response. When you forgive your spouse you experience a letting go of these resentments and negative thinking and begin to re-adjust your view of your spouse to take into account the fact that you have reconciled. This, of course, is easier said than done.

The Impact of Harmful Behaviors

When one spouse harms the marital relationship through some hurtful behavior, feelings are bruised and resentment builds. But there is a deeper impact too; the spouse who is a victim begins to experience what is known as cognitive dissonance. Cognitive dissonance results from an experience—such as betrayal of trust—that doesn't match one's beliefs concerning how another should act toward you. Whereas before there was an assumption of equality between the two people, now there is a perceived power difference. The victim feels "one down" and perceives the perpetrator as "one up." This results in a crisis of trust and a crisis of confidence. You might feel shocked, numb, hurt, or angry, especially if the offending action is a major assault on your core, nonnegotiable values and beliefs. Before the harmful event the victim could trust the spouse and felt equal; after the event there is a real lack of trust, loss of control and a feeling of being one down. In order to get the relationship back on track there is a serious need for both the victim and the offender to talk things through and acknowledge the impact of the harmful behaviors on the marriage.

The Magnitude Gap

Forgiveness is easier said than done. One reason why is the gap in perception on the part of both offenders and victims. Researchers say that offenders tend to perceive their transgressions as less harmful and serious than do victims. In marriages where there is an assumption of equality between both spouses, there is a tendency for each spouse to focus more on their own victim status while over looking their roles as offenders. In other words, we tend to inflate our own sense of hurt while minimizing how we might have hurt the other person. This explains why couples can have serious arguments that go on over time and where both feel that the other is responsible for serious hurt done to the relationship. By focusing only on your role as the victim of hurt, and not taking responsibility for the fact that you can also be an offender, you might be assisting in harming your marital relationship (Forgiveness, McCullough, Pargament, Thoresen, editors, The Guilford Press, New York, 2000, 141).

Benefits and Costs of Forgiveness

If you had to list the benefits and costs to forgiving your spouse what would they be? You might come up with the following costs of forgiveness:

- You would be required to let go of your hurt and bitterness.
- You might have to risk being hurt again.
- You would have to risk being perceived as weak, or as a "doormat."
- You would have to work on seeing the one forgiven in a way that didn't bring up all the past hurt. This can take a lot of work.

On the other hand, if you had to list the benefits of forgiving your spouse you might come up with the following:

- You really could let go of resentment and hurt and move on.
- You would enjoy better physical health. Studies have shown that harboring anger and resentment can lead to serious physical illness like heart disease.
- You might actually have more fun and enjoyment with life.
- You might see some real positive behavior change on part of your spouse.
- Your relationship could improve and deepen.
- Your spouse will cut you some slack and be more likely to forgive you should you become an offender.
- The two of you can spend much more time loving each other rather than resenting each other.

Why It is Hard to Forgive

According to Dr. Fred Luskin of Standford it is hard to forgive because we develop grievance stories that we tell over and over again. These grievance stories just reinforce our victimization, making it more difficult to forgive and let go. The grievance story:

1. Maximizes the hurt done by the offender
2. Makes you into a victim by emphasizing your helplessness and innocence.
3. Keeps the pain and anger inflamed and present to one's consciousness
4. Becomes a template by which a person interprets future slights and grievances, thus giving more power and energy to the original grievance story. (**Forgive For Good, HarperCollins Publishers, 2002) Dr. Fred Luskin www.learningtoforgive.com**

In its worst manifestation, the grievance story turns into a revenge story where the victim has fantasies of striking back, rather than impulses to forgive and let go of hurt.

The Art of Forgiveness

Forgiveness is relational. To forgive means that you are in relationship with someone who has done something to offend you, usually an act that has harmed you at least emotionally. It's possible to forgive someone before that person asks for your forgiveness. Indeed, there have been cases where forgiveness is offered without it even being requested. One thinks of Jesus on the cross forgiving his crucifers right before he died. In a relationship between equals, however, forgiveness involves a process of dialog between the one offending and the victim of the action. That's why forgiveness is an art.

The need to ask for forgiveness and the need to forgive usually arise from a behavior that has hurt in some way the core conditions of marriage: trust, fidelity, respect, safety. Sometimes the action can be minor, like failing to call home to let one's spouse know you have to work late. The behavior can be more serious, like having an affair. And sometimes there is a repetition of minor offenses that creates a pattern of neglect, like staying out consistently after work and not checking in with one's spouse. Think of the core conditions like the bark on a tree. The tree can survive if the bark sustains slight nicks (minor offenses) and even a few major whacks by an ax (major offense), but there will come a time, if the offenses continue, that the bark will be worn away and the tree will die. Forgiveness can restore the bark on our "marriage tree."

The following is a modification of a process of forgiveness developed by Frederick DeBlasio of the University of Maryland. It asks you to address the impact of your behaviors on your marriage while encouraging you to take responsibility for an offense and let go of resentment. The language of "offender" and "victim" will be used to denote the one who does a harmful action and the receiver of that harmful action. To keep things simple we will examine the process using a relatively minor offense, a spouse who works late and does not call home to tell the other about this.

1. Clear statement of the offense

Both of you need to agree on the specific behavior that has caused a disruption in your relationship. Victim: "When you didn't check in with me that you wouldn't be home . . . " Here, the offense is not checking in with one's spouse. In order to go to step two the spouse who didn't check in needs to acknowledge his/her lack of action to check in. Where couples usually get stuck is when the offender minimizes his/her behavior.

2. Connecting feelings with the offending behavior

Victim: ". . . I felt hurt and angry . . . " It is important for the offender to listen carefully to the feelings of the one who has been hurt. This is not easy because the offender might think that the victim is overstating the case; and the offender has a built in tendency to minimize the impact of his or her actions.

3. Specific description of the consequence

Victim: ". . . because I had dinner ready and went to some effort to fix it." Understanding the impact that the offense had on the victim is an essential part of the forgiveness process. The offender needs to understand the consequences of the actions in the specific moment. This will assist in developing an understanding of the hurt suffered by the victim.

4. Validation of victim's position by offending spouse

Offender: "I understand and acknowledge that when I didn't call telling you I wasn't coming home that your were hurt and angry. I understand and acknowledge that you went out of your way to have dinner ready for us." Validation of the victim's position is essential in order to move on and let go. This involves a validation of the victim's feelings as well as how the offending action caused hurt and disruption.

5. Active use of empathy on part of offender to appreciate the position of the victim with reciprocal empathy on the part of the victim

Offender: "If I were in your position I would also be angry with me." Victim: "I'm beginning to understand how you react to work stress. Sometimes you get so focused and forget about me." It is important for the offender to place him or herself in the shoes of the other and experience the side of the victim. At the same time, once the offender demonstrates empathy with the spouse, it is equally important for the spouse to seek to understand any underlying patterns that might be driving the other's behavior. This is true especially if there have been serious issues like an affair, for there are often underlying negative patterns and stressors that need to be explored by either one or both of the spouses.

6. Relationship Building Plan

Offender: "In the future I will . . . do such and such to insure I check in with you. I will also take more responsibility getting organized so that I don't have as much need to work late." This needs to be very specific. It includes both how the offender will take responsibility for making amends and also a behavior change that reassures the victim that the behavior won't be repeated. Also, the victim needs to participate in the construction of this plan especially if the offense is a serious one. The relationship building plan needs to address any patterns of behaviors that might cause the action to be repeated. For instance, many people act differently toward their spouse when they are under increased work stress. They might fail to check in with their spouse. If this is a pattern then the issue will be one of doing better at relieving one's stress as part of the plan. In cases of more serious offences, like affairs, there might be other more serious patterns that cause disruption in how a couple communicates and resolves conflict. When the offense is quite serious, marriage therapy is often needed to address the process of forgiveness and to build a relationship plan that addresses all the issues. As part of the plan the couple needs to address what they will do if the behavior is repeated. For instance, if the behavior is repeated again, is it time to get into marriage counseling?

7. Apology

Offender: "I'm sorry that I have hurt you by not calling." The offender at this point asks for forgiveness. Apologies can be given earlier in the process but they will be believed more deeply if the victim believes that the offender truly understands the impact of the offense on his/her feelings and also the impact of the offense on the relationship.

8. Granting of Forgiveness

Victim: "I forgive you and hope that we can avoid a repeat of this in the future." True forgiveness means letting go of resentment and anger toward the other. This can only happen if a person feels that the issue has been resolved. In serious cases forgiveness can only be given once the victim can trust that the relationship plan has been consistently followed and revised when needed. To forgive means that the victim makes a commitment not to bring up the past action again when the couple argues or has conflict. This is very difficult to do. To truly let go of the resentment and bitterness, and to see one's spouse again as a friend, partner, lover, and companion might take time, but is the goal of forgiveness. To hold onto anger and bitterness begins to make the person a real victim.

Moving On, Moving Forward

Forgiveness, then, works best when we see it as an action that can help us let go of the hurt and anger which keeps us stuck in a victim role. By forgiving you may be able to:

1. Take a hurt less personally
2. Take responsibility for your feelings
3. Become a hero or survivor in the way you tell your story (See **Forgive For Good**)

4. Create clear boundaries that not only protect but which assign responsibility to the offender
5. Give to the offender the responsibility for his/her behavior. Those behaviors say more about him/her than they do about you.
6. Get help in forgiving and/or nurture relationships that foster forgiveness
7. Examine and understand any unenforceable rules (See **Forgive For Good**) that are causing you to feel re-victimized. Unenforceable rules are beliefs about the other person's behaviors, where you wish someone would act different but where you have no power to enforce their behaving the way you want. (People shouldn't lie, life should be fair are just a few examples of unenforceable rules).

A SLICE OF LIFE

Marie and Vince have been married for seven years. Previous to their marriage they lived together for three years. They describe their relationship to their friends as close and are generally satisfied with their marriage. Life is good for them except for one thing that has created at times a great amount of conflict. Marie has at times run up her credit cards to the maximum debt limit and has lied to Vince when she has done so. Just recently a debt collector called Vince at his work and asked when they would pay back the three thousand in credit card debt that was on their cards. This caught Vince completely by surprise since he thought that they were debt free.

At first Marie denied that she had run up the debt, claiming that someone else had stolen her card numbers. Only when Vince secured a credit report did she admit the truth that she was responsible for the debt. She felt truly sorry for her actions and asked for Vince's forgiveness saying that this wouldn't happen again. This time, however, Vince found himself much more hurt and angry with Marie's actions. Further, he didn't believe her when she said that this wouldn't happen again. He felt betrayed and began having thoughts of leaving.

A friend suggested that both of them needed help and gave them the name of counselor. Marie wanted to try counseling but Vince was resistant. He struggled with his hurt and anger over Marie's actions. He eventually agreed to go with her to counseling, making no promises concerning the future.

Awareness In Action

In the above case forgiveness can be more complex than we imagine. Vince has to let go of his resentment and anger toward Marie and might have to look at whether he is taking things too personally.

- Do you think that in order for him to really forgive her he needs to see a change in behavior?
- Does it work that way with the two of you on forgiveness issues?
- Is it easy or difficult for you to forgive? What stops you from forgiving when you're hurt?
- In your experience do the issues of forgiveness involve the core conditions of marriage?
- Have you ever had to go through a forgiveness process as serious as the one described above? Do you think your marriage is in better shape because of your commitment to seek and grant forgiveness?

The Spiritual Dimension: The Forgiving Heart

The real work of marriage begins when you are asked to forgive your spouse. Sometimes forgiveness seems counter-cultural. We are taught from an early age not to let anyone trample on our rights, to defend ourselves at all costs. And there is always the old proverb, "an eye for an eye." Wouldn't we be better off if we just defended ourselves every time our spouse did something hurtful? Yet we know that responding in kind only leads to more hostility and bitterness. But it is so hard to forgive, to let go, to release our resentment.

The root of the word conversion is "metanoia" which means "a change of heart." When we forgive another person who has wronged us we experience a kind of conversion, a change of heart. Resentment and bitterness toward another threaten to turn our hearts to stone. The conversion of forgiveness allows us to have hearts of flesh, strong and vibrant, and full of the life force of God. Forgiveness is not an easy thing to accomplish, it is normal to hold onto resentment and anger out of fear that we will be wronged anew. Forgiveness is a moment of grace where we get in touch with the fact that the offending person is a child of God just like us. Ultimately, forgiveness is a quality of God and when we forgive we assist the creator in the renewal of creation by allowing the creative energies that come from forgiveness to be released.

Answer Honestly then Share....

Forgiveness means....

I can easily forgive myself (True/False)

The difficult thing about forgiving another is....

17

SPIRITUALITY OF MARRIAGE: THE QUEST FOR MEANING AND SIGNIFICANCE

Love is the only sane and
satisfactory answer to
the problem of human
existence.
— ERICH FROMM

The story is told of a young man who, in the days when dragons roamed the land, wished to be a dragon slayer. He apprenticed with a wise battle tested veteran who trained him and prepared him to fight dragons. On the day of his first foray the master told him, "You are now ready to face the enemy. You are prepared as no one else is, except for one thing. You need a magic word that will protect you from the fiercest of dragons." He then whispered this word to him and the young man was off. He found many dragons and was almost reckless in his battles, trusting in the magic word to give him the edge. His reputation increased with every dragon he slew. One day, a rival dragon slayer said to him in contempt, "Ha, you trust your life to that magic word given to you by your master. Don't you realize that it's only a word and that he gave it to you to trick you into believing you could fight dragons?" This caused the young man to become morose and he couldn't bear to fight anymore. He finally went to his master and asked him the truth. Alas, the master confirmed his rival's contention that the word was only meant to make him feel confident. "The important thing," the master said, "is that you trust your skills and fight on." But for the young man this wasn't enough. "Is that all there is, then, my own skills and competency? Do you mean there is nothing more?" To this the master had no reply.

The crisis of the young dragon slayer is a crisis that all of us will face to varying degrees. We want to believe that we are special and unique and that there is a protector "out there" who will see us through the difficult times in our lives. As children we are taught about benevolent figures such as Santa Claus who reward us for being good and bestow gifts on us for our efforts. It comes to no surprise to you that children's notions of God are a variation on the Santa Claus story: God is often seen as a powerful benevolent person who watches over us, protects us, and gives us good things.

There comes a time, however, when you move beyond your childhood images of God and re-appraise how you view God. This might happen when you encounter an event that shakes your sense of security: the death of a friend, parent, or sibling. Or perhaps as you matured through high school or college you got in touch with the central question that faces all believers: why do innocent people suffer if God is all powerful and good? When these experiences happen your sense of personal uniqueness and belief in an all powerful force that will protect you can fall apart, just as it did for the young man in our story. And you might have asked yourself the same question: "Is this all there is to my life, just my own experiences, skills, ambitions and dreams? Is there nothing more that transcends me?

Developing a Spirituality That Can Sustain a Marriage

When you began your journey of marriage you also began a quest for a search for a greater and deeper meaning of life. There is a built in human yearning for something beyond our own experiences, no matter how enriched they are. Saint Augustine's famous saying applies here: "our hearts are restless God until they rest in you."

Research tells us that people who possess a well defined spirituality, and who act on this spirituality by becoming involved in a church or community setting, tend to live longer and feel better about themselves. This is perhaps because the more connected we are with other people and the more we can live out of a set of values, the more we will feel fulfilled. But this begs the question asked above: is there really anything more than just my experiences? To put it more crassly, "What does spirituality do for you anyway?"

In 1995 the American Counseling Association at its Summit on Spirituality defined Spirituality as a *"tendency that is innate and unique to all and moves the individual toward knowledge, love, meaning, peace, hope, transcendence, connectedness, wellness and wholeness"*. At the same time it defined religion as a *"specific organized and codified form through which individuals may express their spirituality"* (*"Spirituality and Counselor Competence: A national Survey of American Counseling Association Members,* Journal of Counseling & Development, Winter 2007 (pp 47-52).) Many people report having a spirituality but not necessarily attending a church, synagogue or temple on a regular basis.

Spirituality, then, speaks to our basic instincts that lead us to reach out to a transcendent power that has the promise of greater knowledge, love, meaning, significance, connectedness and wholeness. This can be expressed in the following instincts about life:

A Sense That Life Is Unfolding points toward Transcendence

It's not that you wake up every day and know that your life has purpose. We humans are purpose seeking animals and we want to believe that somehow all things are being directed toward a goal. You might have felt this when seeking a career or in deciding what direction your life would take. Do you feel this impulse by virtue of the fact that you and your spouse have been drawn together to walk the road of life?

From the perspective of spirituality we can say that God is the unseen force directing the unfolding of life, and that God also calls to the two of you as you walk your road together.

A Sense of Mystery About Yourself and the Created World

There are two parts to a mystery: something that is known or already revealed and something that is yet to be revealed. At every stage of life you encounter yourself as mystery. When you're in grade school you know much about how smart you are and how good you are at sports. But you still have to see how that plays out in high school. When you start your career you know much about yourself, but there is also much that is hidden. Will you be successful, will you be able to fulfill your dreams, will you be happy? The same is true of your marriage. Each of you probably knows the other better than anyone else on this earth, but there still needs to be that area where both of you are seeking to discover the deeper parts of each of yourselves. Without that sense of discovery, and the awareness that there is more to learn about ourselves, life becomes stale and marriage dull.

From the perspective of spirituality we can say that God is experienced whenever we encounter the deeper mystery about ourselves and the world. Living life as a mystery to be explored rather than a problem to be solved places emphasis on inquiring more into what is unknown, both about you and your spouse. When you ponder the phenomenon of yourself, others, and the world you begin to experience the presence of God. A sense of wonder about life itself, about the fact that you can experience deeply, think deeply, and love deeply can lead you to profound transcendent experiences of God.

A Sense of Painful Life Interruptions Which Cry Out For Transcendence

The awareness of the limits of life puts us in touch with the problem of why good people suffer, sometimes quite painfully. The biggest limit is, of course, death. But there are others: loss of health, loss of job, not getting a longed for promotion, or the death of a parent, sibling, or child. Any experience with a true limit brings us up short and reminds us that we are not in control and that what we see happen to others can and probably will happen to us one day. At the same time, realizing our limits gives voice to the cry for transcendence. You see someone you love really suffer and you can do nothing about it and part of you cries out for an answer to life's dilemma: for to really live life means that one day you must surrender control. This cry for transcendence asks for reassurance that somehow one's pain, limit, death will not go for naught, that there will be some sort of return, recovery, resurrection.

In marriage the experience of limits can be very painful, for there comes a time in life with your spouse when you see the negatives as clearly as positives, your own, as well as those of your spouse. You may see, or your spouse may point out your own foibles and failings and how difficult it really is to change. With many couples, it is the experience of parenting that brings them face to face with their limits, as they struggle to deal with problems their children are facing. But in marriage, as in other aspects of life, the crucial crisis comes when one decides to face one's limits instead of running and avoiding them. The embrace and acceptance of limits can be a time of real grace and experience of God's presence even though the experience will initially be a painful one.

Scripture scholar Walter Brueggemann writes about a spiritual pattern that is captured by the Psalms. According to him the Psalms speak to our life experience of going from being comfortably oriented to that of being painfully disoriented and finally to being surprisingly reoriented by the action of God (Praying the Psalms, Walter Bruggeman, Saint Mary's Press, 1984). All of us have had experiences where life was good one day, but then the next something happened to jar us out of our ordinary and somewhat contented experience. It could be the sudden and unexpected death of a loved one, a loss of a job, a problem with a child, or even a revelation of infidelity on the part of our spouse. Whatever the event, we become painfully disoriented as our world turns upside down. We might even feel that God is punishing us or that God has abandoned us. We struggle with disbelief that the event is happening and our life enters a state of disorganization and even chaos. For some, there is a sense that life will never be the same and that the good feelings are gone forever.

The experience of becoming painfully disoriented can create a sense of crisis in your marriage. The spiritual task is to try to work it through, not running from the pain but talking through your feelings and searching for answers. If you're a spiritual person you might find that the familiar prayers and rituals no longer comfort you. The hope, of course, is that somehow in ways you don't expect you will discover that you have been surprisingly reoriented toward life. In a sense, that is the miracle of healing and letting go of intense hurt, anger, and resentment where somehow you are able to let go when before you could not.

A Sense of Being Connected With the Earth and Universe

At the giving of ashes on Ash Wednesday the minister says, "Remember, you are dust and to dust you will return." For some this is a fearful reminder of their death. But it can be so much more, for this ancient formula reminds us that we have come from the earth, belong to it, and will one day return to it. Not only that, but modern cosmologists tell us that the earth itself is composed of collected stardust formed long ago in super novae. Each of us carry in us the stuff of the primal universe and in a very real way we give voice to that primal stuff. Our brains are like quantum organisms, manipulating the molecular level of matter to produce a wonderful symphony of thought and awareness. All of which we take for granted when we debate ideas, go out for a pass in a football game, or swim at the beach. But we are children of the universe, for sure, and perhaps share a common task of experiencing life to the full and striving to allow all people on the earth do so as well.

Concerning your marriage, being connected to the earth can give you and your spouse a grounding in a sense of space. Remember that the Book of Genesis called the first man Adam, which really means, "of the earth." Perhaps the most symbolic thing both of you can do is to celebrate your "earthliness" through the act of sexual intercourse, where in the mingling of seminal and vaginal fluids you are reminded of the primal seas in which life was first created. And, of course, you know that a major goal of sexual intercourse is the procreation of offspring. As spiritual people you give rise to life in all its mystery through conception, just as the earth brings forth in mystery an over abundance of life forms.

TAKING RESPONSIBILITY FOR SPIRITUALITY

Ok, let's say you buy that spirituality is an important aspect in your marriage and that you agree with the above spiritual impulses. Are there any requirements of you? If you're really serious, there are. If you are to continue to name the mystery of God in your life, you need a framework in which to do so. Unfortunately, just the two of you will not do; you need to be attached to a community, which can give you a framework of rituals, values, and routines. In this community you can get connected with like-minded people, share experiences, and help others give voice to their own needs and cry for transcendence. And when you do take responsibility to name your spiritual reality by embracing a framework of community, you will feel more claimed by the transcendent force we call God. This might come in the form of a "conversion" experience but it also could be experienced as just being right. Remember, it's only when we try to go out of ourselves, in this case by embracing a community, that we begin to find ourselves in a deeper way. And this finding of yourself will actually strengthen your marriage and give you unlooked for strength in coping with the many limits and obstacles that come your way.

The Quest For God

Our own spiritual quest, then, embodies the following characteristics, which if we follow and implement, can help sustain our own identity and relationships

- Inquiry basic part. We are open to inquiring about the nature of ourselves, our world, our relationships.
- Open to question and dialog. We start with being open to question and dialog with ourselves, others. Answers come through dialog, not blind obedience to authority
- Conversion of heart important. A change of heart and mindset are the beginning,

being grasped by a reality greater than ourselves leads to understanding our place in the scheme of things.

- Journey, pilgrimage basic image. Life is a journey and we are people on the way, on pilgrimage. Paying attention to how the journey unfolds is very important, as well as with whom we walk.
- Commitment to self development. We are always on the way and in development, the question is whether we make a commitment to continual learning and development, or step off the line, not accepting the call to live life to the whole.
- Compassion, justice basic values. Compassion for others and their suffering is a basic part of this spirituality, also a commitment to restore relationships and the earth in a way that emphasizes healing and wholeness for everyone, not just a few.
- Willingness to forgive. Even though we may be wounded and hurt deeply we commit to a process of forgiveness, realizing that sometimes this is very difficult in any particular moment.
- Life as a mystery, understanding what is revealed, wonder at what is to be revealed. We live life, our lives, as a mystery that is unfolding and we commit to life's continual unfolding.

- Discipleship. We take the stance of disciples, that of learners, sitting at the feet of a transcendent power, learning about ourselves, about others, about our world. We don't seek power over others but power with and for the other.

A Slice of Life

Steve and Missy have been married for twenty-three years. Their oldest is a senior in college, their middle child is nineteen and their youngest is fifteen. When their middle child, Jack was a freshman he began to experiment with drugs. When Steve and Missy found out they intervened as best they could, but Jack's problems only grew worse. He began to have more serious psychological problems which resulted in his being hospitalized when he was seventeen. He was subsequently diagnosed with schizophrenia, something that Steve and Missy were totally unprepared for. It took them nearly a year to stop blaming themselves and they gradually came to realize that his illness is a brain disorder and not the result of poor parenting.

As a result of their son's illness Steve and Missy went through major soul searching. "Why did God let this happen?" was just one question they asked themselves. Up until Jack's diagnosis they were not all that serious about attending a church. But as they began to cope with the impact of his illness they found themselves becoming more involved at a local church. For one thing, it had a support group for parents in their situation.

It also provided a strong youth group for their younger son. It's not that their re-involvement in their local church changed their lives radically. But it did provide them with a context by which they could reorganize their lives as they assisted their middle son to cope with a serious mental illness.

AWARENESS IN ACTION

Life is a journey. But sometimes the highway of life gets a lot steeper and tougher than we are prepared for and life is no longer fun. Spirituality is not magic but it can give us a context in which we can ponder some of the deeper problems of life, like the problem of suffering. It won't take suffering away, but it might help you find some meaning in the suffering you experience.

- Some people have a hard time seeing themselves as "spiritual." Do you see yourself as embracing a spirituality?
- How would you describe this spirituality to a friend? Where do you find the presence of God in your life?
- Do you have specific routines, like prayer time, that help you focus on your spiritual self?
- Are there any other "instincts" or "senses" that you would add that point toward the presence of God in your life and the world?

THE SPIRITUAL DIMENSION: IT'S A WONDERFUL UNIVERSE

The more scientists describe the created universe the more wondrous it seems. The current theory of the Big Bang holds that the universe "erupted" from a microscopic teardrop of energy-matter. Another group of scientists, in their quest for a theory that unites both physics on a large scale with physics on a small scale (quantum physics) have postulated the existence of "strings." Strings, according to this theory, are what the tiniest particles are based on. They are infinitesimally small vibrating strings of energy. These same scientists also postulate that if strings exist then there must be at least seven more dimensions.

These theories boggle the mind and seem as mysterious as the original creation myths of ancient times. While scientists can't make the leap from scientific investigation to the existence of a transcendent being we call God, their discoveries point as much toward the existence of God as away from the existence of God.

Wouldn't it be interesting if the rhythm of your marital love and the music the two of you make together throughout your married life were in some strange way related to the music of the "strings" of matter? Does your dance of intimacy reflect the dance of the universe? Aren't you curious to find out?

Answer Honestly then Share....

My questions about the existence of God are....

I get in touch with my spirituality/God by...

When I think of someone who reminds me of spirituality I think of .....

Made in the USA
San Bernardino, CA
02 June 2017